4-1-00

To DON —

Best on all your

personal journeys

[signature]

JOURNEY THROUGH DIVORCE

JOURNEY THROUGH DIVORCE

Five Stages toward Recovery

Harvey A. Rosenstock, M.D.
Judith D. Rosenstock, Ph.D.
Janet Weiner

INSIGHT BOOKS

Human Sciences Press, Inc.
72 Fifth Avenue
New York, N.Y. 10011-8004

Printed in the United States of America
987654321

Library of Congress Cataloging-in-Publication Data

Rosenstock, Harvey A.
  Journey through divorce.

  Bibliography: p.
  Includes index.
  1. Divorce. I. Rosenstock, Judith D. II. Weiner, Janet,
1930–   . III. Title.
HQ814.R67   1988   306.8'9   87-22574
ISBN 0-89885-403-2

CONTENTS

To all who have known loss firsthand, and to our children Amara, Aaron, Benjamin, Deborah and Marc—for whom God has blessed the Journey.

JDR, HAR

ACKNOWLEDGMENTS

No journey through grief is ever taken alone. Ours were not exceptions. There were special people who cared when we didn't, cried when we couldn't, and loved when we wouldn't.

To Dru who urged the poetry, to our parents—Pearl and Jacob Naistadt, Leona Rosenstock, and Arnold Rosenstock, of blessed memory—whose teachings and support sustained us; to all our relatives, especially Laura and Dan and Aunt Clara; and to our many friends—especially Monica and Roger, Joanne, Richard, Sandy and Jerry, Jackie, Carol Lee and Maurice, and Sheldon—we thank you from our heart. You were all there for us.

We would also like to thank Janet and Jerry Weiner who began the awesome process of creating organization out of our ideas by asking the salient questions that needed answering. We also express our gratitude to Janet Neff and Bonnie Bakal who tirelessly worked to bring the many revisions of this manuscript into its final form. Special thanks to May Dikeman for her fine copyediting of the manuscript.

INTRODUCTION

Divorce is a juncture in the life cycle that directly affects tens of thousands in America daily and, by extension—parents, relatives, friends and associates—hundreds of thousands.

Divorce always ushers in Winter, regardless of the season. In many ways it's an early death on the life cycle. However, most divorced people have the potential on their own to journey through this winter and embrace an increasingly productive Spring. *Journey through Divorce* is dedicated to helping facilitate the necessary move away from disruption and disorganization and even drudgery—stemming from unavoidable loss—toward a life pattern that embodies understanding, increased self-confidence, self-worth, and productivity. This will be associated with good feelings, fun, and positive expectations.

Journey through Divorce looks at divorce as a predictable and identifiable series of stages—Denial, Depression, Anger, Resolution, and Recovery—each with its own characteristic challenges, passage through which indicates forward progress. Because in actuality the movement through a given stage so often is best described by feeling tones, short poems are presented which are the direct renderings from the real journey of one of the authors. No one person travels the identical path of another with its own oscillations—forward and back—but the general route is nonetheless strikingly and uncannily predictable.

Divorce may be compared to object loss and to death itself because, in a marital relationship there is not only the husband and wife but there is also the marriage. It is a tripartite arrangement. The marriage is lost. There is the death of the marriage. To some extent there are losses to each individual—plans, hopes, and dreams that will never be realized—but the main loss is of the third entity. As in dealing with death, there are certain stages through which each survivor must pass.

By identifying with the stages and the feelings contained within each, one may find solace, definition, and meaning; reassurance, hope, and direction imbue what may otherwise seem a labyrinth through fear and failure.

Journey through Divorce shares a series of candidly expressed and identifiable experiences that give meaning and structure to the chaotic world of Divorce. Depiction of each stage is followed by an illustrative case history of a different couple's journey through that stage.

The psychiatric commentary that follows each poem probes and further interprets the emotions conveyed. These poetic expressions have proved helpful in various settings, including therapy by clinicians. It is also written for those family members and friends who want to better understand, support, and help the victims of divorce.

Judith Rosenstock has written every poem as she went through each of the stages in her own painful transition from married to single life. Her poetry flowed from the heart at a time when she was fighting for emotional survival. It was a time when she experienced the immensity and urgency of the divorce phenomenon, from the grievous process of separation and dissolution, to gradual self-revelation and fulfillment.

Journey, born of many poignant moments, is a message of optimism with roadmaps leading toward the ultimate rejoicing that heralds a more autonomous and brighter future.

As Judith finally exults in her poem *Triumph;* (Recovery)
  The world looks hopeful
  It's good to survive
  My destiny is *mine*
   to create and direct
  Thank God I'm alive.

          H.A.R.

PROLOGUE

My poetry flows
    from my
    pain
I cry inside
    and the words
    tumble out
Releasing the tension
    easing the agony
    quieting my tormented
    soul

The words deliver a
    sense of reality
    a meaning to
    my turmoil
    a definition to my
    hurt

It focuses my
    despair

It generates my
feelings
and ultimately
eases
the pain
and restores balance
and harmony
My poetry
sustains me.

1

STAGE ONE

Denial

SEPARATION

Can we live together?
Can we live apart?

Can we share our moments
    our past
    our future
    without each other?
Can our love survive?

Can we wake up in the morning
    to a cold bed,
    a lonely room
    an empty closet?
Can our love survive?

Can we separate ourselves
    and remain whole?
Or are we whole because of
    our togetherness?
Can our love survive?

> Can we be creative
>   fulfilled
>   and fulfilling
>   without each other?
> Can our love survive?
>
> Can we live together?
> Can we live apart?

SEPARATION

The first flashes of reality are flooding the heart. Still in love, but admitting that the foundation of the marriage is badly shaken, another plea is made. The bonds of tradition, intimacy, and continuity will break if there is a separation—so an attempt is made to offer reasons to stay together.

Still denying that the divorce may occur, questions are posed: Is the risk really worth it to you? Do you know what you are doing? Are you really going to let this happen? There is the minimally expressed hope that there will be a reconsideration, and he will stay.

It is still much safer to believe that this is little more than a brief storm through one of life's many rough passages, rather than a well thought out ending to a marriage. This form of denial—an abstract pleading for the reification of the marriage—is a very normal and expectable phase.

Repression early in the journey through divorce predictably lends itself to various forms of pleadings; it should therefore be no surprise to find oneself enveloped in quid pro quo appeals. These are characterized by: "I have always given and sacrificed so that we could walk the final steps together;" "We've been through so much, so why now can't we realize our dreams and together share our children?" "I have never loved anyone so completely, so deeply—and never could again; let me really prove it to you."

In this way denial lays the predicate for the emerging feelings of shock and disbelief. The ego, though far from shatterproof, will not now be quite so vulnerable.

A Plea

I have been mistaken
I loved you—I thought you knew
I tried so many ways to show you
But you say I never asked.

I have never loved another
I could never love another
I love you so completely
I was too casual.

I want to grow old with you
I want to share our dreams
I want to share our children
I want to share our love.

A Plea

This poem represents an unwillingness to accept the possibility that the marriage will not survive. It denies the fact and attempts to assuage the pain by begging forgiveness for real or imagined transgressions. Shock, denial, and fear all blend together to preserve the vows and stave off divorce.

Love was given forever, never to be broken, never to be destroyed. Loyalty was unquestionable; it came with the vows. And with that love, loyalty, and devotion came the right to a lifetime together.

To keep the marriage intact and deny the possibility of ever having to live alone, supplication becomes a painful part of daily life. The preservation of fantasy impels the promise to alter anything that was unsatisfactory. "It was all *my* fault." At this point no cost is too much. The coat of dignity is shed.

Denial allows one to consider the sacrifice of the self in order to guarantee the perpetuation of the marriage. Any diminution of the self provokes still further disequilibrium. This is beyond the conscious reasoning of the individual at this time.

Because self-dignity is not a priority compared to preserving the fantasies of many years' accumulation, any sacrifice is justifiable. Supplications take on diverse guises. The desire to accommodate and change any unacceptable traits—whether imaginary or real—guides all actions. "I can be different. I can be a totally different person."

The psyche still remains too vulnerable to consider the notion of divorce. The acceptance of the "I'm *not* OK" (ego dystonic) position prompts one to plea-bargain regardless of personal pride.

FREEDOM

I know the fear that
    races through the body
Freedom is a precious
    commodity
    hard to find
    easy to lose.

Yet freedom can become a fantasy
For life without a significant other
Can be a lonely, empty place
Simply filled with actions
    not with compassion
        caring
        understanding and
        love.

So keep the freedom
Treasure it—but
Choose carefully
    or "freedom"
will imprison you.

FREEDOM

This is yet another strategy—a more complex one—for keeping the marital relationship intact. Though it appears to be a willingness to allow him to individuate and have his freedom, it is in fact a maneuver of paradoxical intent. This is a dire warning that he will regret his quest for freedom. Freedom is incapacitating.

Be forewarned. The strategy implies that the world is a forlorn and insecure environment. Without the love and companionship that their marriage can provide he will become depressed and confined in an aloneness of his own making. There is an intimation of the threat that by the time freedom is savored and ultimately imprisons him, she will be gone!

The invitation that Freedom really presents is the freedom to fantasize but not actually leave. Think about freedom, fantasize about it, and sample it sparingly; but don't yield to it too much— please.

In the earliest stages of the journey through divorce resistance to accept a change in the status quo, i.e., to even fathom the dissolution of the marriage contract is commonplace. Mental machinations run amok with schemata for reversing the threat. These include intrapsychic bargaining, pleading, self-castigation, and reaction formation.

Reaction formation is one of the more primitive defense mechanisms whereby feelings which are too painful for the conscious ego are repressed. In their stead are formulated ideas which are diametrically opposite, for example, "He doesn't *really* want to leave, it will be too devastating for him, he'll miss me, and then he'll regret it." Despite the extraordinary efforts to avert the separation, the house becomes divided.

ONCE

Once we loved together
Our hearts, our bodies
   blended as one.
Today we are separated
   by the untamed passions
   of man—
Now I love alone.

ONCE

Once you loved him and he loved you—now you love alone. This provides a narrow escape hatch for him to leave; yet keeps open the opportunity for him to come back to you. Unrecognized co-dependency issues obscure the reality of a new life-style.

Loving alone is both a fear and a fact. There is still no indication that there has been any emotional letting go, only the physical removal of the spouse from the home. The bonds of love refuse to be broken, even if dignity and loss of self-respect are the toll extracted to keep that love alive.

In the denial phase the shock, disbelief, and fear appear overwhelming. The sense of loss paralyzes the ability to disengage from the marital relationship. Even the actual separation does not, cannot sever that love.

Co-dependency issues prolong the denial stage and foster resistance. Like other mechanisms of defense, resistance serves to keep from conscious awareness not only undesirable feelings but also premature insights.

All the psychiatric defense mechanisms notwithstanding, the brutal reality is that living alone is extant. This is what prevails. It is impossible to avoid the decisions that have to be made as an uncoupled person. As more and more obligatory choices are made—such as moving, child visitation, and budgeting—denial necessarily weakens.

YESTERDAY

Yesterday I loved as an
    innocent
Today I love in confusion.

Yesterday I believed in a man
Today I believe in no one.

Yesterday my identity was
    us

Today my identity is
  me.

Yesterday my tomorrows
  seemed filled
Today my tomorrows
  can't be imagined.

Yesterday I felt loved
  and secure
Today I feel rejected
  and abandoned.

Yesterday I had hope
Today I need hope.

YESTERDAY

Although denial is still the omnipresent force, there is a shadow of recognition of the reality of divorce. Identity becomes a critical issue since the once permanent dyadic relationship is being unquestionably threatened. Issues of self-awareness and self-identity begin to surface, unresolved, hanging heavily in the present.

Tomorrow is no longer a safe place, a vision of ". . . and they lived happily ever after" land. The security of a well planned coupled life no longer provides protection and nurturance. There no longer seems to be any security or love on which to depend. Rejection and abandonment can no longer be pushed away—they force through a brutally shattered identity that fumbles for hope to carry on with the tasks of life.

Virtually everyone goes through this process, whether it lasts for days, months, or years. The premonition that something is about to be irrevocably lost is becoming impossible to deny. Despair begins to push denial aside as the journey through divorce continues by shutting out the yesterdays and admitting the prospect of the unimaginable tomorrows.

A Confession

I came to you a child
 entrusted you with my deepest feelings
 my greatest desires
 my love.

I thought the gift I gave you needed
 no nurturing—my being was its
 continual reaffirmation
I was wrong.

Today I come to you a woman
I entrust you still with my
 deepest feelings
 my greatest desires
 my love.

But I will tend the gift, renewing my
 vows of affection to you so
 they can continue to grow
You were right.

A Confession

The offerings that were brought to the marriage were not enough. Even though they were all one person had to give to another, they were rebuffed. Perhaps if the love were more *mature*, or more demonstrative, or more unpossessive, or more of anything, it could still be saved.

For someone in denial, human self-sacrifice on the altar of divorce is reasonable if it will prevent the marriage from dissolving. It is not unusual to bargain with the devil to ensure safety and security from the unknown. In fact, such negotiations provide a mechanism to avoid facing the reality and moving forward with life. There will be time *later* to deal with the future; this allows a period of readjustment and rethinking.

At this point, depending on the degree of victimization and

subjugation, self-confidence may have plunged to its lowest ebb. One may feel unsure of *everything*, including intellect, looks, and sexual desirability. Not uncommonly, one becomes consumed with ruminations typified by "If only I had done what he wanted" and, "I should have realized what he meant." The denial stage can become fraught with the "If onlys" and the "I should haves."

At the same time, the internal struggle is just beginning. The naive girl must make way for the emerging woman whose very existence she wants to deny. The fear of being alone pushes away the woman, who is aware and knowing, and clings to the innocence and illusions of the past.

CASE HISTORY I

Donald, age 38, and Carol, age 35, had been married for 15 years and had four children ranging in age from 3 to 13 when Carol demanded a trial separation. Carol indicated a need to establish her own identity separate and distinct from that of her husband, a successful professional. Donald reasoned that his best strategy to effect a permanent reconciliation was to acquiesce amicably to Carol's ultimatums. During the ensuing months, well-meaning friends and relatives informed Donald that Carol was not in fact pursuing her own identity, but an affair with a mutual acquaintance. Donald refused to credit these reports and defended Carol. Thus Donald denied the dissolution of his marriage.

Throughout the separation and the eventual divorce proceedings Donald maintained a determination that Carol's need for space and separate identity be met and that, thereafter, the marriage as a matter of course would be reconstituted. His denial of reality and his cleaving to the illusion that an ongoing breach was only temporary immobilized him. This immobilization took the form of intense child rearing and professional activities at the cost of attempting new patterns of socialization. Between the separation and the granting of the divorce decree which encompassed nearly 2 years, Donald steadfastly refused to see any other woman. During this denial phase, Donald willingly allowed himself to be manipulated by Carol into performing all the chores that were to her convenience in running the nuclear household in hope of entrenching his position.

An event finally occurred which gave Donald a foothold on reality—a friend informed him of Carol's impending engagement. This shock pierced the illusion of her need for a separate identity and catapulted Donald into beginning the journey through divorce.

Commentary:

In the clinical experience of the authors, the need to move on to the subsequent stages is critical in that it permits divorce victims to refashion and retool their lives for dynamic continuance. Those who are unable to move past the denial stage may live the rest of their lives *married in absentia*. These people rarely reach their full potential in another loving relationship or as fully actualized individuals. Such individuals clearly need therapeutic intervention to catalyze moving toward resolution and recovery.

Denial of the dissolution of a marriage is a natural response. It forms a protective armor, allowing the self-designated victim an opportunity to be shielded from the searing reality of the marriage's termination and the resumption of a single life. However, when denial is prolonged, the process of dealing with the loss and moving forward is critically delayed.

For those who perfect the stage of denial, the necessity to journey forward becomes more threatening than the initial loss. The desire to avoid further pain inadvertently prolongs the intensity of the anguish rather than its abatement.

SUMMARY AND SUGGESTIONS

Denial is usually a defensive measure, part of the body's natural healing process, and is replaced by early realization and a queasy acceptance of the end of a marriage. Denial allows us to *examine the pieces* of the puzzle of our new circumstance, accepting only the aspects that make life even remotely palatable. For most people, reality ultimately takes over, and gradually they come to see their romantic illusions for what they are. Slowly, they begin to recognize the fact that the marriage has indeed ended, and they are now living single.

Everyone goes through the stage of early realization and acceptance in the denial phase. If you don't recognize the reality of what your situation is, then you have ceased to connect with the outside world. In order that you don't get swept up in a torrent of emotions beyond your control, you must establish a supportive network of people to help you. There is no way to make this an agreeable passage, but it is not a time to withdraw from living or to pull away from your friends. This is a time to suffer, reevaluate, and grow.

During the period of shock and disbelief, time is held in abeyance until reality can take over. At this point, you may be able to recognize that you have needs, though you may not be able to determine what they are.

Denial in a time frame can be as brief as several months, or go on for as many as 5, 10, 20 years, or more. Unless the loss is recognized, progress to the next stages in a natural sequence may be aborted. The danger is that you never reach stages of resolution, and therefore never fully embrace the knowledge that life really is worth living.

The following suggestions are offered to facilitate the recognition of denial and the forward movement to the next, predictable stages:

1. Deliberately seek out and stay in touch with one or more friends. The tendency to withdraw at this stage may falsely signal that you don't want contact from close friends. Communication needs to remain open.

2. Recreational activities must be pursued. Attending a movie with a friend can be an important release. Caution should be taken in choice. Avoid those dealing with divorce, child custody, death, or other forms of loss. Such dramatizations would only mirror the despair.

3. Keep a journal. Feelings and thoughts that clamor for expression can find release in a personal diary. Express your feelings about your sense of loss, grief, pain, anger, hate, and even love. This will prove a tremendous catharsis that will carry you through the divorce journey.

4. Frequent bookstores and libraries; read all you can on the subject. How others have dealt with similar losses can help you understand your own situation.

5. Talk to other people who are also undergoing a divorce or who have already been there. The problems and experiences you share may make them seem less overwhelming and less terrifying.

6. Maintain sound nutrition and proper sleep habits. In this period of numbness, it's too easy to avoid eating properly because of lack of appetite. For those given to binge eating in times of stress, separate yourself from the food sources in favor of a productive activity, especially one that will occupy your hands. Do not take hypnotics to regulate sleep without the advice of a professional. To do so would be to invite new problems.

7. Treat yourself to something: new cosmetics, hairstyle, clothing, hobby equipment, home decorating item that expresses your own individual taste.

8. Listen to relaxing music. Avoid lyrics that remind you of how it is to be in love.

9. Use the telephone. Call someone when you need a receptive ear and a shoulder to lean on. Also be sure to ask what's happening with *them*.

10. Don't underestimate the support you can get from sympathetic sources. If you have family, try to surround yourself with them. Usually they will take their cue from you on what to talk about. Relatives who "told you so," who've got the picture all wrong, who have a gift for saying the wrong thing, still are the people who *always* care about you. In their anxiety they may blunder, just as you may, but their anxiety is to help you, and *you* can help them to help. They "don't know what to *say*," but what they *feel* is for you.

11. If you have young children, approach someone to help you for awhile with them. The very relatives who were out of their depth in trying to discuss your situation with you may be endlessly resourceful in helping with your children. It is important to recognize that when your own needs are so acute, you may not be able to

provide for your children as you would like. Children, who always have great dependency demands, cannot comprehend your compromised ability to consistently meet all of their needs.

12. Know that professional help is available. Seek it out if you feel the need. In many instances group therapy can be sustaining. Through the group you can benefit from altruism, universality, and peer support. This interactive process will allow you to fortify your own strengths, recapture lost self-esteem, and reaffirm the intactness of your thinking processes. If you are anchored to an impasse, a therapist will help you to accept the reality of the end of the marriage and at the same time show how life for you has a new beginning.

Suggestions for friends and relatives who want to help during the denial stage:

1. Be there for support. It isn't always necessary to say anything specific at this time. Listening nonjudgmentally is fundamental.

2. Respect that this is the early stage of mourning for your friend or relative. She or he is lamenting an irretrievable loss.

3. Ask if there is anything you can do to make the activities of daily living easier. You could, for example, take the children to an activity. You could take your friend or relative shopping or do the shopping in their stead.

4. Tell the person that she or he is fine, that going through something as terrible and sad as divorce does not make them a different person to you.

5. Don't be afraid to call after 11 P.M. This is the time when the divorcing spouse is most alone and depressed. Therefore, the ringing telephone might be the most welcoming, reassuring signal that someone really cares.

2

STAGE TWO

Depression

I Don't Want to Be Alone

Oh, God—
    I don't want to be
      alone

I feel engulfed
    by space
Shouting but
    unheard
Crying but
    unseen
Shaking but
    untouched
God help me
    to accept
    my aloneness
    not fight it
    to find an inner
      peace

But right now
at this tortured
moment in time

I don't want to be
alone
Oh God—
I don't want to be
alone

I DON'T WANT TO BE ALONE

Feelings of pain and anguish surface, and are not to be denied. *I Don't Want to Be Alone* describes coming face to face with one's rawest emotions. Thrust into a world of darkness and emptiness and unable to create a scenario that would provide an alternative setting, this poem cleaves to the pathos of depression.

The awareness of being alone plunges one into the stage of depression. Feeling utterly rejected and alone is to contemplate what death would be like. The fear of living and the fear of dying are joined at this moment.

This stage of depression is a time for mourning—a time for tears. So often in a divorce the loss is seen as a *failure* rather than the *death* of a commitment and partnership. When the confused societal messages mix with the agonies of separation there is little space for healing. Loss must involve mourning and a recognition that life has changed and the different life must continue.

EVERYTHING IS GONE

How can I explain the hurt inside
I am afraid the wound will never
heal
The pain will never cease
The tears will never stop.

I want so much from life
I want to share my thoughts
    to share my days
    to share my nights
I want to love and be loved
    in return.

Can the hurt heal without another love
Can the wound heal without
    another love
Can the pain cease without another
    love
Will the tears stop without
    another love?

I want so much from life
I have so much to give.

EVERYTHING IS GONE

As depression becomes the more prevailing emotional symptom, there is a concurrent fear that everything is lost. There is likewise an inability to imagine a less painful world. The sheer pain of loss obliterates memories of anything good that may have been achieved during the marital relationship.

Embodied in this poem is the subliminal hope that the wayward spouse will realize his loss and seek to return to his partner. At the same time, the bone-deep resonance of the pain denotes that this will never happen.

The recognition that loss has occurred despite all efforts to refuse its admission into conscious awareness means that depressive feelings will be accepted into intrapsychic life. This also means that the work of mourning for the loss can proceed.

Depression describes both an affective state characterized by feelings of sadness, futility, hopelessness, and discouragement and by a change in motoric activity characterized by lassitude and anergy. Even the most routine task can seem monumental. Getting up in the morning is a major victory for a depressed person. Pessimism permeates all thoughts. Decision making is burdensome. Tension and anxiety can mount to the point that the felt depressive feelings appear secondary. This state may even manifest in the form of querulousness and fractiousness where virtually anything is perceived as adversarial.

As depression becomes more progressive, there can be a deterioration in dress and personal hygiene. Apathy becomes the keynote. Thinking becomes labored as the ability to concentrate and apply oneself is temporarily compromised. Suicidal fantasies which may occur at this time should always be assessed by a professional.

Depression can also be somatically expressed through gastrointestinal dysfunction, loss of appetite, insomnia, early morning awakening, cluster headaches, and tremulousness. Many people may be tempted to focus on diagnosing an organic basis for the somatic complaints to circumvent confronting the true depression. This relentless pursuit of a diagnosis other than depression is costly in terms of time, psychic pain, and—if needed—life-sustaining professional treatment.

To My Son—To My Daughter

Your life is not as
   I would
   have had it

I wanted you to be
   loved
  in one house
   with
  Mommy *and* Daddy

Instead Daddy lives far away
  You go to new schools
   Make new friends
    Have new people in your family

I ache for your need for
    stability
    structure
    safety and
    security

I will try to provide you
    with the
    love you need
      to
    garner the
      things we
    held so dear

Love me
Trust me
    as I love you.

               Mommy

To My Son—To My Daughter

This poem reflects the deep and profound loss onto the other victims of divorce—the children. The needs that are expressed are for *everybody*—not only the children but also the mother.

Fear of meeting the unknown, and of the struggle to provide a stable, loving environment against great odds, catapults the victim into recognizing the needs of others. This serves to mobilize the remaining family members towards a future—albeit a questionable one.

Stagnation and immobilization which define the more profound depths of depression are in part nullified by the recognition that the children have needs that this parent can best provide. Parenting drives can become powerful organizers which not only serve to neutralize the psychomotor paralysis that has taken hold but which can mobilize the innate abilities of this parent and focus the energy on forward movement.

The needs of the children begin to pierce depression's mist. The children regain priority in daily thoughts and feelings. Parenting without a partner has become a reality.

WHAT'S WAITING FOR ME?

What's waiting for me
Out there in front of me
Bitter disappointments or
        joyful days and nights?

What's waiting for me
Tomorrows full of sadness
        and woes or
Tomorrows filled with
        happiness and delight?

What's waiting for me
        at the end of the tunnel
Knowledge that I loved
        and loved for naught or
The creation of new loves
        wrought from the despairs
        of loss?

What's waiting for me?

WHAT'S WAITING FOR ME?

Questions come crowding one after another. The underlying question is, will there ever be happiness again? The impossibility of seeing into the future is fearful. In fact, the pain of the recent past makes the prospect ahead seem all the more foreboding.

Marriage came with a guarantee—or so it seemed. Now there are not only no guarantees, but is there even a future? Having invested so much feeling and energy into a relationship that failed begets a reluctance to invest into an unknown tomorrow. This hesitancy contributes to the incapacitation which is such a familiar part of depression. Planning for the next 24 hours and carrying this agenda through to completion can be many times more salutary than extended abstract speculation on the long-term future. To refuse to plan concretely for the foreseeable future is to give depression no boundary and to remain tethered to past losses.

THOUGHTS FROM A WEDDING

Strange to go to a wedding
        thoughts racing of my own
        twelve years ago
Questions of one someday in the
        future . . .

Till death do us part
        or till one of us leaves?
For better or worse
        or till we give up?
To have and to hold
        or till we grow bored?

Was I naive
        or did I just believe?

Strange to go to a wedding
        the thoughts will continue
        to race.

THOUGHTS FROM A WEDDING

The life cycle continues for others—only provoking ruminations over recent disillusionments and disappointments. To be left at the altar of marriage with unconcluded vows redefines the feelings of loss and abandonment.

Still, evidences of future-directed thinking begin to surface as thoughts stir of another marriage, also unconcluded. Finally, a hope emerges in the midst of patent sorrows and rejections.

Ambivalence typifies this substage of depression. How to survive depression and continue with the life cycle are questions cyclically that reemerge. The catalyst may be an event reminding one that the life cycle goes on for others. Reality dictates that there *is* a future; furthermore, that treacherous waters must be navigated, not only now but again in times to come. It is delusory to expect that authentic survival is not won over sorrow and loss of varying degrees. With this understanding comes the ability to find pleasure vicariously in someone else's good fortune, while simultaneously beginning to surmount one's own feelings of sorrow and rejection.

MOVING DAY

I cried today
    tears welling up and spilling
    over refusing to stop
I cried for the love I once had
    the future that might
    have been
    the family we once were
    the home this once was.

I cried and my crying
    paralyzed me from
    packing away the remaining
    items of our lives together
I cried to stop the pain and
I cried to remember the pain.

But ultimately I cried
    at the final transformation
    of a home back into a house

And a wife back into an
    unmarried woman.

God how I cried.

MOVING DAY

    The despair in breaking up the final ties that unite a family, unite a couple, and unite a person may be the worst. To divide possessions and sort through memories tears apart the once intact home and also the person whose home it was. There are objects you don't know what to do with: a book he once was excited about, but wouldn't want now. Neither of you want it, but you can't throw it away.

    When you dissolve a marriage, at first it's still theoretical. But, when you actually move out of the house, there breaks the realization that you will never go back. The home symbolizes the family—the move represents its loss.

    A move under *pleasant* circumstances evokes sadness, memories, and loss. A move precipitated by divorce deepens the depression and underscores the grief. Tears must be shed, feelings must be allowed to surface, and the pain, however permeative, must be purged. There is no longer any room for denial, hope, or even wishing, as reality asserts its iron grip and pushes us forward. All that is left is the overwhelming sense of loss—loss of identity, home, and the life we once knew.

SEPARATION REVISITED

    The pains of separation don't
        disappear
They lie under the surface
        ready to emerge at the
        slightest provocation.
I think of the friends I'll never
        see again

> The places we'll never
>   visit together
> The death of the man
>   I knew, loved, and trusted.
> If only the ghost of the man
>   did not haunt my daily life
> I could free myself from
>   the past
> And enter into my future.

SEPARATION REVISITED

The chasm between what was and what is becomes more gaping with each passing day. A life once joined by common interests, beliefs, and friends is torn apart. Few friends are able to bridge this abyss.

Ultimately the spouse is thrown off the cliff—a fallen idol smashed to bits and pieces. His restoration and subsequent intrusions into her world only exacerbate the anger and infect the wound. To wipe him out is now the main objective.

Unlike the mourning that accompanies death—*divorce shuttles back and forth* between real and unreal with calls and visits from the soon-to-be ex-spouse. There is no space to adjust to the loss without constant trespass from the source of that pain. Mourning is a prolonged, often interrupted, rarely understood process. The grief is abraded by continual reminders of their life together. The depression moves forward as she purges him from the exalted place in her life and attempts to move onward.

CASE HISTORY II

Marian, age 52, and Jack, age 60, had been married for 31 years and had one daughter, age 27, when Jack abruptly terminated the marriage and left the States. For a brief period of time Marian could neither believe nor accept her status as a single woman. Within 6 weeks she began to withdraw from her usual social activities, ceased church-related volunteer work, and refused to babysit for her grandson. Marian found it difficult to eat. She lost weight and easily became fatigued. She would burst into tears over trivial matters—the breaking of a teacup. As part of her general withdrawal and self-imposed isolation, she would spend hours sleeping. Then her daughter persuaded Marian to enter therapy.

Clinically, Marian presented as a significantly depressed, middle-aged woman who felt that her remaining future had been stolen from her. She could see no value in herself in terms of being able to do anything productive again. She rationalized that her husband's abrupt leaving was a confirmation of her global inadequacies.

Marian required some months of individual and group psychotherapy coupled with antidepressant medication to be able to reconceptualize what had actually occurred. This brought her back into touch with her own talents and her role as a loving mother, grandmother, sister, aunt, and friend. She accepted herself as a sentient person who had much love to give. She moved on more quickly through the subsequent stages of divorce no longer immobilized by her depression.

Commentary:

Although the multidimensional loss in divorce produces symptoms of sadness and other depressive traits, not everyone actually suffers a clinical depression such as Marian. For those unable to navigate it, it is this stage that can prove the most threatening to long-term survival. Therapy at this stage is essential if one finds oneself at a prolonged impasse which extends into weeks or months. Often one is blind as to when to seek help, particularly at this juncture. A critical guideline would be if several close friends and/or relatives encourage seeking outside help. This is where consultation with a minister, family doctor, or other mental health professional can be beneficial and create an approach to encompass the marital loss.

SUMMARY AND SUGGESTIONS

Depression is a syndrome with both affective and motoric traits with varying degrees of expression. Depression also represents movement out of the stage of denial and toward the stage of anger. Depression means that awareness of loss is to some extent tolerable to the conscious ego. Working through the meaning of the losses becomes possible. Even planning for a future without a partner has its rudimentary beginning in this stage.

The end of this stage is manifested by increasing energy, more organized planning for self and children, recognizing that one can contribute constructively to others, and the emerging ability to express anger outward.

The following suggestions are offered to help navigate through the stage of depression.

1. Recognize that depression is not only predictable, but that it is a *normal* part of working through the entire experience. Realize that you are going through something that others have experienced, and understand that depression is an unavoidable part of the journey.
2. Choose at least one person to serve as a confidant. Share your feelings freely.
3. Find an activity that draws you out from being alone at home, simply mulling things over. Whatever activity you choose, it should be pleasurable, commensurate with your interests, abilities, or things you have enjoyed all along. Enroll in a course, attend a show or concert, entertain friends.
4. Continue to maintain your health; get rest, exercise, and proper nutrition.
5. Learn to relax your whole body and mind.
6. Get a pet. You need only consider your own preference, not a spouse's attitude or allergy. Having a pet gives you the incentive you need to get moving each day instead of wallowing in your depressed state; something to touch.
7. Decorate or redecorate your home or apartment, following your *own* taste, applying *your* favorite colors.

Especially redo your bedroom, because that's the place where intimate memories were made.

Suggestions for friends and relatives who want to help during the depression stage.

1. Reaffirm that you are always available. Make it a point that your friend is not left alone excessively.
2. Extend luncheon and/or dinner invitations. Help fill in some of the empty spaces with friendship.
3. Help with the children.
4. Express your sorrow about the divorce. A simple hug or pat can be incredibly supportive.
5. Do call in the evening. This is still appreciated in this phase.
6. Seek the opinion and advice of your friend, putting your question earnestly. This is a reassurance that she still has something worthwhile to contribute to others, and is needed.
7. Don't avoid her because you feel inadequate or uncomfortable, and "don't want to get caught in the middle." Your avoidance could only hurt and cause more pain. Just your presence can be salutory.
8. Don't interrupt if your friend repeats a story. Allow her to satisfy the need to ventilate her unhappiness.
9. Don't criticize the ex-spouse. This would only make the friend more defensive while inhibiting her working through separation.
10. Don't rush the process. This can't be done. You can best serve by being patient, understanding, helpful, supportive, and by offering security.

3

STAGE THREE

Anger

ANGER WELLS UP

Love wells up inside me
     searching for a way out
     searching for a place to go
     searching for a reason.

Anger wells up inside me
     searching for a way out
     searching for a place to go
     needing no reason

Fear wells up inside me
     searching for a way out
     searching for a place to go
     having plenty of reason

Hope wells up inside me
     searching for a way out
     searching for a place to go
     creating the reason.

ANGER WELLS UP

The earliest admission of anger and its need for release is found in *Anger Wells Up*. This represents moving on to the next stage in the journey through divorce. Expression and ventilation of the hostile feelings are far more important than a labored analysis of the source of the anger at this point.

As an emotion, anger serves to *catalyze other feelings* and work through the pain of abandonment and rejection. It provides the avenue to *safely inspect* the remnants of feelings so brutalized in the divorce process—buffering the zone of depression, yet still knowing all of the sadness.

There are many *positive* aspects to anger. Just recognizing its existence means that anger is no longer too threatening to be permitted into conscious awareness. This in turn signals that the psyche is in the process of marshaling its forces to deal with the obligate ventilation of the anger to come. Further, the preparation for the anticipated catharsis also confirms the existence of an emerging sense of *security*.

DESTRUCTION OF LOVE

Lies destroy
Deceit destroys
Angry words destroy—

Passion destroys
Cruelties destroy
Lust destroys—

Greed destroys
Bitter deeds destroy
Pride destroys—

But most of all
You destroy love.

DESTRUCTION OF LOVE

Once it seemed totally impossible to conceive of a life without his love—now anger emerges to suppress and ultimately destroy that loving bond. His actions are now identified and labeled, and then reexperienced. Each replay sharpens the growing realization that *he* is *not* OK—in fact, he is quite despicable.

Anger rages—love dies.

The anger is not only intensifying but is becoming more polarized. Psychiatrically, this is a *healthy and natural* process. Being afraid to display anger and aggression is in fact a denial of the whole divorce process. Expressing anger globally is only somewhat less of a denial. With the anger appropriately focused, one no longer needs to bend under the dead weight of repressed feelings.

AM I BITTER?

Bitter? Am I bitter?
    Why? Because he left me
    at the peak of his career
    before I ascended mine?

Jealous? Am I jealous?
    Why? Because he left me
    for another woman—even
    though I loved and trusted
    him so completely?

Angry? Am I angry?
    Why? Because he left me
    and was cruel and unkind?

Hurt? Am I hurt?
    Why? Because I respected
    and admired him so fully
    and he betrayed me?

> Happy? Am I happy?
>   Why? Because I am free
>   from a man who made me
>   bitter, jealous, angry, and hurt—
>
> You bet I am!

AM I BITTER?

This poem fully depicts the opposite range of emotions of the earlier groveling, self-pitying, cowering, woman-child, clinging wildly to her crumbling past. Both emotions are real and both are needed. Bitter can taste sweet, as indeed it does when poured on the villainized spouse. Each action he takes is savored for its palliative conduciveness to recognizing him for the *bastard* he became—rather than the saint that he once was.

Catharsis—the intentional articulation of repressed experiences with their concomitant feeling tones—is not dominant. This recognition and expression of anger allows for the release of many other pent up emotions, including jealousy, bitterness, hurt, and qualified happiness.

With the source of the anger identified and the catharsis in progress, there is new energy available for understanding the consequences of the divorce on the victims. Yesterday's paralyzing depression has given way to today's actualization.

THE SPLINTERED FAMILY

> Vocabulary words—
>   that's all they used to be to me
>   divorce
>   custody
>   visitation
>   stepparent
> Now they dictate my life
>   no longer a wife
>   now an ex

You can end a marriage
But how do you end the need
    to be with your children?
To watch them every day
    hold them
    hug them
    tell them you love them
    kiss them goodnight

I don't know yet
The question haunts and torments me—
    kids—
        good night
        sweet dreams
        and
        God bless you,

        Mommy

THE SPLINTERED FAMILY

Anger is not solely directed at the personal loss of a husband, lover, confidant, and friend—but now the reality of a profound personal loss becomes evident. Suddenly a full-time mother is forced through the legal process to relinquish her children into their father's possession for visitation. Part-time parenting is one more indignity left to resolve.

The meaning of loss is expanded to include not only the private, personal rejection of a spouse, but also the sad splintering of the once sacred, indivisible nuclear family. This leads to inexorable changes in role definition.

Rage is expressed at a system that legalizes the divorce process and the regulation of parenting time. Lawyers, judges, and courts are seen as powerful interlopers. In fact, the whole divorce process has careened out of control. The result is maddening.

It is almost universal to regard any mandated intervention by others as adversarial. This presents a secondary source of anger which must also be confronted and neutralized. *Recognition* of the anger, *identification* of the source, and subsequent *ventilation* of the associated affect are effective steps for channeling this anger.

Additional sources of anger continue to be identified as the details of the new life-style unfold: those hours and days when the children are with the other parents; those unwanted times alone; solitary dinners; holidays unshared.

THE WOUNDED CHILDREN

Of all the pains and hurts
    I have felt
The deepest of all
    is the suffering
    of the children

So confused
So angry
So abused
    by you

How do I ease
    the agony
Still the internal
    struggle
    to help them accept you as you are
    not as you were
Gentle the turbulence
    of their wounded
        hearts

My children
    I love you so

I cry with you
I cry for you
I suffer, too
I only wanted joy in
        your lives

I'm sorry—
    I love you
    I love you
    I love you

                    Mommy

THE WOUNDED CHILDREN

Anger continues to surge as the lives of the children—now identified victims of divorce—are more closely examined. Needing to assist them through these turbulent times, the anger is polarized at the parent that smashed the intact family and wounded the babies.

Wounded Children expresses how hard it is to assuage the pain of the children when the personal pain is so keen. In order to prevent this pain from occluding the path, the depression has to be contained. Mother actively reaches out to her children. The indignities of divorce are the fallout after the storm of separation. The driving force is the overwhelming sense of ultimate responsibility.

What is occurring at this point is the reorganization of the fragmented nuclear family. Problems are more clearly delineated. Priorities are beginning to be formulated. The new future, while still in its nascent state, is perceptible. Boundaries are changing; the world dimension is expanding. Self-reflection will continue for some time, but with an enhanced scope to see and appreciate affects other than depression and anger.

YUK YUK
(LAUGHTER, IT FEELS SO GOOD)

I know I'm getting better
    when I can giggle
    and laugh
in the midst of despair

Did you know that the first
    three letters of your
    license plate are SYN
Did I hear she threw a
    pie in your pompous
    face at a party—Oh that
    felt good

Can you believe an oil slick
    washed over your romantic
    beach front?

Did I see you get a speeding ticket
    rushing off together?

It's nice to know I can
    hear the humor—
    see the poetic justice
    and taste the fruits
    of that pie.

YUK YUK
(LAUGHTER, IT FEELS SO GOOD)

Delightful, joyful, vengeful humor! Ironies and strange twists of fate are now incorporated into a master plan of revenge by a more Supreme Being than any mere mortal. Sarcastic humor releases angry energy—but it's so wonderful to laugh again.

Anger can actively be dissipated through sharply focused humorous comments. This is a universal phenomenon, generally reflecting a higher order of cognitive functioning. Laser-accurate quips can be a source of tremendous relief while at the same time giving the impression that one is going on with life: Dependency is undergoing a well-earned metamorphosis into real autonomy.

Anger can also effectively and safely be dissipated in a passive way. Here imagination and fantasy reign supreme. In one's mind terrible and tragic occurrences befall the former spouse. The scenarios may have fairy-tale endings: Pitiful, woebegone derelicts come crawling back, craving forgiveness from a now omnipotent woman who is in full charge of her own life. Revenge themes flood the psyche. The only limiting factor is the boundless imagination of a bright, creative mind.

Discovering humor in the ambiance of daily life represents still another forward step in the journey through divorce. No longer needing to depend on contrived scenarios, one is now able to appreciate a more balanced view of the external world. Consciously seeking out a comedic quality in today's world with its infinite permutations is to know that progress is ongoing.

While rich fantasies are both healthy and soothing, the realization that life itself metes out ironies and tragedies that exempt no one is the true elixir. Humor is a prism through which manifold emotions can be refracted and resolved.

CASE HISTORY III

Randy and Brenda, ages 34 and 32 respectively, had been married for 8 years when they began "drifting apart." Randy seemed to find more reasons to go on business trips for longer periods. Another year passed before Brenda confronted Randy about the length of time he was spending away from her and their two children. This confrontation resulted in what was at first an "amicable" separation.

However, Brenda became increasingly angry at the realization of Randy's leaving, and Randy became angry at Brenda for having pressed issues to the point that a divorce was inevitable. For Randy this also meant an incalculable loss in terms of his perceived business image and community standing. Over the next year and a half there followed numerous court battles and hearings with referees over child custody issues and property settlements. The anger experienced by both Brenda and Randy was played out in the arena of the courtroom at tremendous financial and emotional expense. The rage became so intense that they themselves lost sight of the more serious issues of the welfare and well-being of their own children. In fact, they unconsciously used their children to carry on the war between them, until one of the children became so symptomatic as to be referred for psychiatric consultation.

Whereas neither Brenda nor Randy would at any point have considered marriage therapy, they were both receptive to consultation on behalf of their seven-year-old son. In the course of treating the child, Randy and Brenda were forced to identify the sources of their own anger and its impact on the development of their own children. This helped mobilize a more reasonable approach to the resolution of the anger. Settlement on issues of property division and child custody followed quickly thereafter. With therapy, they were able to modify their relationship to one of parents in separate households. They became committed to communicating with each other more rationally and more effectively to allow for the most normal growth and development of their children.

Commentary:

The case of Randy and Brenda is illustrative of anger occurring simultaneously in both spouses. This stage can be most damaging for the children involved. Further, the finality of the divorce decree does not guarantee the end of the anger. Many years later there can be recurring episodes of child custody and child support fights, and courtroom conflicts over the interpretations of divorce decree language, or the same strife waged between the spouses outside the courtroom. These incidents are representative of unresolved issues of anger.

If one spouse is in the denial or depression stage and the monied spouse is in the anger stage, efforts must be taken to protect the more vulnerable spouse. The selection of legal representation is crucial to insure the most equitable disposition of property, child support issues, and custody issues. The more vulnerable spouse could be taken such advantage of at this stage that recovery would be unnecessarily and painfully prolonged.

For example, it is tempting for a woman in the denial stage to *acquiesce* to her husband's wishes in the hope that her passivity will reduce antagonism on his part. She fails to take seriously the reality of the divorce and her future needs because of her clinging to the denial stage associated with the irrational hope of a reconciliation. It is critical to *separate out the anger from the issues of property settlement and child custody* to protect the rights of all those involved.

SUMMARY AND SUGGESTIONS

Successfully processing anger entails its recognition, definition, and constructive dissipation. Techniques for accomplishing these steps include such active means as dialogue with others, focusing energies toward selected projects, and discovering and articulating humor in the ambiance of daily life.

Passive means for the dissipation of anger are also efficacious and include mental imaging of situations involving the other spouse in varied states of supplication before the now omnipotent ex-wife. ("I was really crazy for a while." "Well, whatever, things have changed for *me* now.") Fantasies become a rich source of relief and release.

Signs that the stage of anger has been successfully navigated include (1) a more balanced view of the events in the outside world; (2) realistic delineation of problems to be resolved; (3) prioritization of goals; (4) rediscovering humor in the trivia of daily life; and the reemergence of energy and resolve to engage beyond the boundaries of the self.

The following are suggestions for dealing with anger:

1. Dissipate anger in an active way such as manipulating inanimate objects. Hitting tennis balls against a wall, kneading dough or clay, painting with brush or palette knife, and playing a musical instrument are examples.
2. Active and passive involvement with sports activities is always helpful—the more active, the more useful. Play softball, jog, walk, stroll, bike, or dance. Spectator sports such as professional football, boxing, and wrestling can be effective outlets, depending on the extent of emotional involvement. Even soap operas can be a source of vicarious release through identification with the plight of the protagonists.
3. Read books or attend movies where your anger can be

projected. Rage at the villain; cheer with the crowd for the hero or heroine.

4. If you have theatrical skills, get involved with a production. Read scripts, attend try-outs, learn lines, understudy—even wash the flats!

5. Continue to write in a journal. Angry thoughts are better expressed than left to fester and smoulder.

6. Write down all the epithets you can think of—alphabetically.

7. Take some time off from child rearing. Your angriest moments are the most difficult to control and not displace on your children. Give yourself some space, preferably with friends and relatives.

8. Drawing is also an effective means for ventilating feelings. No artistic talent is required.

9. When anger remains intense despite efforts to identify sources and dissipate the attendant emotions, it is reasonable to consider psychotherapy, especially group therapy. Group process allows for camaraderie, introspection, and catharsis in a controlled and ameliorative setting.

Suggestions for friends and relatives:

1. Don't patronize. Allow your friend the opportunity to ventilate angry feelings and emotions without saying, "I know somebody who had things worse," or "You could have been older . . ."

2. Encourage your friend to participate in activities that help dissipate anger (see above list).

3. Make certain your friend is not alone for holidays and former anniversaries.

4. Provide time off from parenting responsibilities. If the anger is being child-directed, help your friend to recognize the need to rechannel this negative energy.

5. Understand that anger, depression, and denial are not entirely separate entities with coinciding boundaries—but rather a flux of emotions that vacillate. One day

your friend may be angry and the next day depressed.

6. Humor is healing. A good sense of fun, a joke, may be an antidote to anger. Help your friend smile again.

7. Reassure your friend that rejection by one person is not tantamount to rejection by the human race.

4

STAGE FOUR

Resolution

FINDING MY NEW ROOTS

I thought home was with my parents
     home of my childhood
     home of my roots
     home of my memories

But I realize I am home
     home here with my children
     home here with my friends
     home with my newfound security

I am truly at peace
     our life together a memory
     my recent past—my despair
     my todays—finally happy
     my tomorrows—worth living for

I am home.

FINDING MY NEW ROOTS

Moving does not create a home—a home is created out of acceptance, love, and nurturance. Finally, a new life can be established replete with all the identifiable ingredients that made childhood such a loving and secure part of the life cycle. Now the divorced person can point with pride to a similar environment—this time, self-made.

Finding My Roots testifies to the establishment of a new equilibrium, founded again on the strength of genuine relationships. Home is *the dwelling of the autonomous self.* Home is where you are with your children. Home is where your friends and your children's friends congregate in mutual support. Home is where roots grow and security blossoms.

This poem also depicts the normal and predictable regressive tugs that are common at moments of crisis and transition. At these times it is natural to reflect on the most secure memories in order to find strength to deal with what lies ahead. Thinking of being cared for by one's own parents and recalling one's roots are favorite reflections on which to anchor life's next epoch.

THE BRASS RING
(I GOT IT!)

The waiting is over now
   having accomplished another goal
This one I did amidst
     great odds
     great fears
     great frustrations

To achieve something through perseverance,
     personal strength and
     pure determination
Makes the success very sweet
Very sweet indeed.

THE BRASS RING
(I GOT IT!)

When the first laps of the journey unfolded, success at any venture seemed improbable if not impossible. As the healing process takes place and goal setting becomes realistic, personal achievements take on a new and exciting dimension.

The stage of resolution is now in full force. Denial is past history. Depression is only a remnant. Anger is no longer an enemy but rather a recurrent emotion with readily recognizable triggers. Coping skills are sufficiently well honed to deal with the challenges extant.

Thus, the withdrawal of support the former significant other offered is diminished in direct proportion to the degree of success accomplished by the emergent single person. Success breeds success.

TOO SOON

My love is under the surface
Searching for an object
Looking for an outlet
Trying to surge forward.

Yet my intellect says too soon
     too soon
     to be vulnerable
     to trust
     to care
     to share
Too soon.

Too soon to love again
Suppress the urges
It's just too soon.

Too Soon

Perhaps nothing is as frightening as exposing healing wounds to sources of new pain and irritation. Yet the need to reconnect with others, particularly men, begins to emerge. However tentatively, one starts to look around, and the process begins.

"Rejection as a woman" needs to be conquered.

Having been totally rejected as a sexual being, the evidence of being an attractive woman will need to be built up. The damaged ego must collect its own tokens. This takes alertness.

Early in the stage of resolution additional emotional needs come into awareness. The need to love and be loved as a mature adult is recognized, if only fleetingly. Vulnerability carries with it the risk of repeating the whole cycle. For now, this is too daunting.

The stage of resolution also portends an expectation of positive outcome, presupposing deliberate planning. Competent coping is a tool in your armamentarium. You are now increasingly confident that any challenge can be met.

In Balance

The clouds have dispersed
    before me
Exposing the expansive
    blue sky

The snow has melted at
    long last
Allowing the daffodils and
    tulips to burst forth
    from the earth

The wind has ceased
    its relentless howling
Calming to a soothing breeze
    gentling the morning air

Nature like humanity
    returns to peace

In Balance

Everything is in its place again. Before, the forces of nature were an onslaught; now they are benign and beautiful. There is a new optimism which is part of the emerging autonomy. By allowing the processes of pain and healing to take place—processes which are inherent in the nature of life—the body will heal itself and close the emotional wound.

An important part of the therapeutic process is not to abort innate restorative forces. A pierced ear, even after a decade, will attempt to close the hole that has daily been stuck through even if nothing is done but ceasing to probe it. Faith that all will work out is more tenable because so much has already come into balance since those fearful beginnings when survival itself was so precarious.

Time is also appreciated as a healer—but only if it is coupled with an inner desire to survive and see another spring. Nature will always have its seasons; likewise recovery permits human beings to gain peace. Harmony exists once again. Homeostasis has resumed.

I'm Still Alive

I can see the growth
I can taste the joys
I can smell the success
I can hear the music
I can feel the strength

Life's five senses are more
        precious to me now
I want to revel in it all
I want to enjoy what life
        will allow
I want memories to cherish
        and recall
Damn it—I want it all!!

I'M STILL ALIVE

A lust to taste all the sweetness of life suffuses this poem. Here is a frenzy to make up for lost time. Now is for sharing, caring, and setting up a fresh rhythm, a new beat. An omnivorous hunger demands appeasement and refuses to go unfilled.

At some point in the successful journey through divorce a conscious decision is made to reach out for personal growth and to sample everything life has to offer. To be aware of this decision is to know that you are well on your way through the resolution stage. Recovery is nearly an inevitability.

Making memories is a technique utilized by the authors (HAR, JDR) with some success to consciously plan for a memory bank of joyful experiences on which to build the edifice of the future. This entails making decisions to engage in activities that have every likelihood of yielding pleasure and enjoyment. Because we all carry with us the videotapes of our total life experiences, loading the memory quotient in favor of the positive can only serve to catalyze more in the same category. The obverse being equally true, leaving all to chance seems unnecessarily self-sacrificial.

SIGNPOSTS

When pleasant thoughts
    outweigh the bad
When happy times
    overshadow the sad
When calm and tranquility
    replace agitation and anger
When peaceful sleeps
    replace fitful nights
You know you are
    becoming yourself at last.

SIGNPOSTS

Every trip counts on signposts along the route to ensure safe passage to the destination. All too often, in the journey through divorce, travel on uncharted roads compounds the fear of the unknown. It is a relief to spot signals that confirm that this journey is finally headed in the right direction. We're getting there!

When a child asks "Are we having fun yet?" he is really asking adults in his life to read the signposts. He is depending on their leadership for guidance on how to interpret and respond to the environment. The adult who has suffered the crises of divorce and its regressions also depends on external signals for a critical reading of the territory. Direction can also be picked up from the interpretations and translations of trusted friends and relatives, as well as from one's own educated ego.

I Am Trying

I am trying
    trying to recenter myself
    trying to rediscover myself
    trying to reeducate myself

I don't want to depend
    on him for my happiness
    on him for my verification
    on him for being OK

It's not easy
    I'm afraid to like myself
    I'm afraid to become too confident
    I'm afraid to be really alone

But I am trying
I am trying.

I Am Trying

A more mature sense of optimism pervades this poem. Everything is admittedly not resolved, but there is a new hope and determination to try for an authentic solo existence. Becoming a woman who is fully individuated and autonomous will not be easy—but it is worth the attempt. Life *will* go on.

At this stage it is advisable not to be afraid of candor. Frustrations need to be articulated. If uncertainty is taking over, it's often useful to reflect on the progress that has been made from the outset. Reviewing the signposts for each stage achieved on the journey thus far can be reassuring and inspiring: *I've come this far.*

I Am Trying also restates personal goals; the rediscovery and reeducation of the self and the push for further autonomy, free from dependency on the former spouse for declarations of happiness and affirmation. ("Are we having fun yet?")

How Much Longer?

You can still inflict pain
I am not immune to your
        arrows of revenge
Each time I think I am strong
        enough to withstand anything
        from you
You spot my vulnerability
        aim and hit.

I was doing so well tonight
Free from you
Becoming me
And then your arrow hit home.

How much longer do I need to
        fight
When will I be free from you
        and your cruel power—
God grant me my freedom
Grant me back my life.

How Much Longer?

Arrows—a word, a look—can still pierce the moments of peace and open the wounds. The spot that should have calloused over turns out still to be thin-skinned. But ever-increasing bands of experience give the sense of a freedom evolving into true independence. In fact, an impatience is stirring to move on with life—to see what's around the bend.

For each year of marriage there were thousands of shared experiences that resulted in multidimensional bonding. Though separation and divorce may have been legally effected, the memories—conscious and uconscious—cannot simply be annihilated. Throughout the journey there will be flareups of painful recall. Whether the event was pleasant or unpleasant, it sears the memory. These flashbacks are not tokens of failure. They are an inevitable part of the working through that has been ongoing for months.

No relationship is all bad or all good. If it were, the whole divorce process would be painless. It is precisely because marriages and relationships of duration span the range of human emotions that disengagement is so arduous and the path so serpiginous.

How Much Longer laments the vulnerabilities that remain; at the same time it confirms that once the relationship was sufficiently close to risk intimate self-disclosure.

In moving forward, it is a sound idea to *treasure* the memories of closeness rather than to denounce them as "not *real*." Compartmentalize in your memory bank the best times. Instead of trying to erase it all, try to see what was warm and intimate as proof of your own capabilities to be close again to another person.

I'M ALMOST WHERE I WANT TO BE

> I want to be loved
> I want to feel the
>   security of caring
> the pleasure of
>   pleasing
> the joy of
>   being
>
> I fear the unknown
> but the known

will not provide the
shelter of love
the protection of concern
the peace of security

So I will pull away
free myself from you
create the space
and wait for it
to fill.

I'M ALMOST WHERE I WANT TO BE

Resolution begins to contemplate preparation for seeing new people. Some ex-spouses pathologically cling to the old relationship in order to avoid even mentally envisioning a new relationship.

In this poem, courage is summoned to sever the old bonds that chain one to an impasse and to suffer the doubts and longings of the "wait." The reward is space for fresh hopes and dreams. The once ravaged ego is now sufficiently sturdy to meet life's newest challenge—a new person.

"Going out" is a unique situation among the newly divorced. There is the awkwardness of meeting someone and getting acquainted—a seemingly insurmountable task. The decisions on what to do and where to go appear endless. There is the question of whether the children should be introduced. There is the issue of whether and when to have sex. All this adds up to great insecurity and risk taking.

Here, letting go means taking the chance of getting involved. This is a tentative, almost passive beginning. Clearly, there are no safeguards on this part of the journey; but there is the inner strength that brought one to this point. For some, seeking a new life and perhaps a new love is to venture out once again among the living.

When you have reached the point that you are considering "seeing someone" and are considering the variables over which you have full control, you can take pride in telling yourself, "I'm almost where I want to be."

ALL IS NOT FORGIVEN

I find I hate you
    I thought it would
      diminish
    but late at night
      alone in my
      room
    alone in my
      house
I find I hate you.

You promised so much
    You deceived so
      greatly
    You left me
      so completely
      so utterly
      so alone

Even though I am finding
      happiness
      love and I hope
      a beautiful future

I still find I hate you
    for you
      wounded me
      like a
      hunter wounds
        a bird

And because I trusted that
      you would always
      love and nurture
        me
I still find that
    I hate you.

ALL IS NOT FORGIVEN

All Is Not Forgiven (which is OK) voices the feelings of intense hatred that recur from time to time throughout the Journey. This is psychiatrically different from the amorphous acrimony characteristic of the early phase of the stage of anger. Here the hurt individual simultaneously targets her anger, identifies her reasons for her feelings, and states her conclusions. No apologies are tendered. Only a direct announcement of fact is offered: "I still find that I hate you."

This expression of pinpointed hostility is delivered without halting the work of resolution which dominates this stage. It may be discouraging to have flashbacks of anger and depression in the resolution stage; however, these are natural and normal as experiences and emotions collide. The critical factor in determining the acceptability of this kind of temporary relapse is its duration. Brief eruptions of rage occur without warning at this juncture. Even homicidal wishes are not uncommon. Central to the work of resolution is the theme that life goes on, undeterred by occasional backslidings.

The resolution stage always contains elements of hope and positive expectation—but sometimes in proximity to such incongruous feelings as contempt and bitterness. The key point is that eventual recovery is recognized as inevitable. By its nature, progress is not uniform in pace. But the overall direction is a forward one.

LIFE ALONE

Life alone is not always
        lonely
Life alone is not always
        empty
Life alone is not always
        frightening

There are times when
        I realize that
        I control my destiny

I control my future
I control my life

I have reached a
    glorious moment
of being by myself
    not afraid
    not crying
    not wounded
But not wanting it to
    last beyond a moment.

LIFE ALONE

Life alone is no longer the nadir of hopelessness that it once seemed. To be able to enjoy moments of self-reflection without sensing danger or hurt is a sign of new strength. This signals that the process of resolution is well underway.

This poem also illustrates that the "glorious moment" of feeling in control of one's own destiny may still be only a fleeting one. The work of resolution continues. Aloneness and loneliness really are different: The former is a neutral statement of factual status; the latter is a description of painful affect associated with this status.

Life Alone also speaks to the recognition and limited acceptance of the change in role definition that has been ongoing since the journey began. Being single no longer means a leap in the dark. Rather, being single means not having to share the credit for one's own accomplishments. As strength is gathered and as success is scored, confidence builds.

Having a copilot on life's journey is looked for term of the human condition. But what is reassuring is to know that the pilot at the controls is fully credentialed to carry on with decisions of destiny solo—and for an indeterminate period, if need be.

FRIENDSHIP

A friend knows you are hurting
    without your needing to cry out

A friend knows your pain
 without your complaining

A friend knows when to listen
 and is not afraid to be silent

A friend knows when to speak
 and is not afraid to talk

A friend cares with a compassion
 that goes beyond words and
 beyond silences
 to that empty and scarred
 wound in your heart to
 help caress the pain and
 ease the sorrow

A friend is you.

FRIENDSHIP

Divorce often results in the death of valued friendships and longstanding relationships. Few are able to withstand the emotional storms that strain the links that once joined couple to couple, individual to individual, friend to friend. But never were friendships so valued as those that broke through the barriers of grief and brooding and brought much needed comfort and encouragement.

From the psychiatric perspective, many concepts are only first truly understood by the appreciation of their opposites. Happiness and peace that are wrought out of pain and chaos become a lifetime treasure.

Until now, friends were needed, enjoyed, and used, but far too seldom really acknowledged. This stage of resolution fully recognizes the concept of human kindness and loyalty and the value of a true friend. The dependency is then no longer one-way, but is based on an honest appraisal of mutual friendship: caring and sharing.

In this stage the woman reaches out to *return* the friendship that has sustained her during the traumatic days and nights. A rebalancing shift is taking place. She is able to resume the role of *being* a friend.

MOM AND DAD

When I was a child I used
　　to lie in bed and
　　think of you both
Afraid that anything might
　　hurt the mother and father
　　that protected and nurtured me
Aware that I was a child of love.

When I was a teenager I used
　　to lie in bed and think
　　of you both
Afraid that you might give
　　me more freedom than I
　　really wanted
Aware that I was a child of love.

As a young adult I used
　　to lie in bed and think
　　of you both
Afraid that you wouldn't be
　　there when I needed you
　　or that I was too grown-up to ask
Aware that I was a child of love.

Yesterday I lay in bed
　　and thought of you both
Afraid that even though you
　　were there, and I had asked
　　that you could no longer help
Aware that I was a child of love.

Tonight I lay in bed
　　thinking of you both

Afraid to have you leave
    knowing for all of us you must
Aware that I am still a child of love.

Tomorrow I will lie in bed
    thinking of you both
Afraid to disappoint you
    I love you both so much
Well aware that I will always be
    a child of love.

MOM AND DAD

The stage of resolution is also an opportunity to place in perspective one's coordinates on the life cycle in terms of personal history, family values, and moral legacy. Surviving the divorce is reminiscent of the law of biology which states that children survive their parents.

Many questions are faced: Will I be able to really take care of myself? Will I be able to take care of my children? Am I an adult? Can I resume my adult life? What if I get hurt again?

An inventory is taken of those who are closest and of the support they give. "Who are my friends?" is asked repeatedly.

Psychologically, it is natural to place someone in the parenting role. This can be an actual parent, a sibling, or a close friend. The essential element is that at least *one* other empathetic human being is, at least temporarily, allowed a *rescuing* role. This therapeutically powerful move gives respite from the potentially destructive fears of having to solve everything single-handedly. Sociologists point out that dyadic relationships have much more impact than the sum of the individual units.

The security and safety that Mom and Dad represented during each developmental epoch from childhood through adulthood can now also come from selected and trusted confidants. Armed with such support, even the uncertainties of the realistic future hold more potential than the best fantasy of the past.

A Plea to My Parents

Why can't you understand
    It hurts to keep explaining
    I can't have the kids
        whenever I want

I understand your confusion
    they're mine
    I'm their mother
    I want them
        here ·
        today
        now
            too

But divorce decrees
    my time
        and
    his time
And you'll have to understand
    that sometimes
    I won't have them
    even when you travel miles
        to see us.

Why can't you understand
    It hurts to keep explaining
You see I hardly understand
    myself.

A Plea to My Parents

The divorce is *never over* when children are involved—if the endpoint sought is perfect compromise. Grandparents will be predictably disappointed because their time and input have been artificially diminished by legally imposed restrictions in the name of equality.

"The court ruled—" will not assuage the frustration of "Why can't we see our grandchildren?" No amount of explanation is sufficient to placate the grandparents ("But it won't seem like Thanksgiving") and other close family members who no longer enjoy ad libitum contact with the children. More attention than ever before must be paid to quality of time with the children. Alloted days and hours become increasingly precious. Acting on this principle, the children may enjoy more enriching experiences than they might have before the divorce.

Parents are advised, however, not to compete. Concentrate on planning for what you and your children especially like to do together, not on one-upping the other parent. Children of course will play such rivalry for all it's worth, but know that they are missing out on what they need most—attention paid *them,* as people, not pawns in a long-drawn out contest.

THE ABSENT PRESENCE

They say don't worry,
        don't give it a second thought
We'll always be your parents
You'll always be our child

But the disintegration begins
        as the fabric frays
        and the blood lines flow
And the truth emerges
        I was only a daughter-in-law

Good bye, Mom
Good bye, Dad
In case I don't call
        Happy birthday for all the future years
In case I can't come
Feel the absent presence those times
        for tears.

THE ABSENT PRESENCE

The stage of resolution is not completed until the issue of the newly defined relationship with the extended family of the spouse is addressed. Disappointment will be compounded if the expectation is that nothing will change. Initial offerings and re-assurances ("Nobody will ever mean to us what you have meant") often are made in the heat of crisis and don't stand up to the test of time.

The extent of life's losses becomes patently clear as months turn into years. Loyalties clash and love lines queue up—leaving people standing alone. It becomes increasingly apparent that the family system moves to recapture its own, and even the strongest in-law ties become attenuated or severed.

The Absent Presence reminds you to prepare for the failure of certain long-standing traditions to be sustained—at least in the form once cherished. The stage of resolution allows for dealing with this special separation with its own losses. "Happy birthday for all those future years" means Godspeed for dear ones from whose course yours has been rerouted. Already conscious defense mechanisms are in place to begin to accept the antici-pated losses of future privileged contact: "In case I can't come. . ." Recovery as a separate person is now in process.

THE LAST TEARDROP

The tears have dried up
   leaving behind
      the tracks of
         despair
  across the shadows
     of my face
The tears washed away
     the turmoil and the anger
     rolling on the pillow
     beneath my head
The tears removed him from
     within
     slowly

agonizing tear by tear
until he was gone
    and there was room
for life and happiness
    and love
    to enter
    my world.

THE LAST TEARDROP

Just as flashes of anger can occur in the stages of resolution and recovery, so can tears well up spontaneously, without this denoting regression. Tears here are a sign of psychiatric purging—necessary and normal.

The Last Teardrop depicts the tears slowly and agonizingly purging the last traces of love, desire, and codependency from the heart. Crying is not an indulgence in self-pity. It is a painful catharsis that allows emotions to emerge and be set in their proper perspective. Seen in this light, crying is a positive force that gives full vent to feelings that have been bottled up.

This poem alludes to the quiet, ruminating pain that ultimately spills onto the lonely pillow. When you can identify with these moments, it is essential to remember that without such intervals of solitude to reflect on days past, and on life's promising future, the journey could not continue. The release could not be completed.

CASE HISTORY IV

Lisa and Jonathan, both 28, decided after 4 years of marriage to go their separate ways. Each was more dedicated to developing a career than having a family. Lisa journeyed through the stages of denial, depression, and anger, and most of resolution before seeking therapy. She presented herself as a well-educated, articulate, attractive, and career-oriented young woman. Although Lisa was active both professionally and socially, she was oppressed by a sense of purposelessness to it all. She saw herself doing "the right things," but didn't see any clear-cut endpoint. Lisa's recounting of her life-style revealed an almost frenzied approach to reengaging the world. She was dating several men; she had joined several singles groups, a professional women's group, two academically oriented organizations in which she held office, and was taking a course in photography. Lisa identified all these activities as providing two avenues for herself: first to meet people; second, to continue personal self-improvement. She also admitted to recurring, though brief fantasies of her previous marriage and its dissolution. She was unable to understand this phenomenon.

After initial psychiatric consultation it was mutually decided to place her in group therapy with other professional young adults. During the course of treatment Lisa was better able to understand that in fact she had not completed her journey through the stages of divorce but entered therapy only in the stage of early resolution. The fact that she saw herself nonpolarized helped her identify the unlabeled anxiety that she felt because of the lack of total resolution of her problems. She learned that by diffusing her energies into so many activities she was denying herself the opportunity to introspect. Group therapy helped her identify more reasonable goals for herself both of immediate and intermediate term. It was of interest that in order to become a member of a regularly scheduled group therapy she had to eliminate some of her diverse activities. This process itself helped Lisa focus on the issues that were most important to her.

Lisa's dating also became an expressed area of concern. She admitted to a fear of social and sexual intimacies following her divorce from Jonathan. Because of her initial need to be affirmed as a woman in the fullest sense, Lisa allowed herself to become sexually vulnerable. Following one unsatisfactory sexual experience she sought many other sexual relationships, usually with married men, in order to obtain that elusive sense of affirmation without the risk of obligation. This was not entirely conscious to her until it was explored in the process of therapy. Short-lived regressive flashbacks to the earlier stages of divorce were understood by Lisa as being not only normal, but part of the working-through of her feelings and gaining a sense of purpose.

Commentary:

The stage of resolution is often mistaken for recovery by those in its throes. This stage allows the individual opportunities to express self-awareness, self-discovery, and self-fulfillment. Like Lisa, people at this point are able to do some goal setting and take the risks attached. One may tend to overextend one's self and ultimately lose the opportunity to fully individuate. This is the stage that provides the groundwork for meeting new friends and recognizing long-standing, true friends.

Single parents find the resolution stage somewhat more complex as they must simultaneously meet the needs of dependent children. These parents often add to the list of activities such organizations as Parents Without Partners and fathers' rights and mothers' rights groups. These organizations can provide both support and an avenue for catharsis for the single parent.

Further, single parents are faced with the added task of having to find guiltless time periods to allow for their own personal development. This stage becomes identifiable as a problem when the parent is so frenzied that there is in fact little time or opportunity to engage in appropriate child-rearing activities. Again, one must avoid the trap of too much activity and not enough private time to internalize new social changes.

SUMMARY AND SUGGESTIONS

This penultimate stage of the journey through divorce focuses on gaining something substantive out of momentary bursts of depressive and angry feelings. There is greater awareness and acceptance of what it means to live independently. Energy and strength are reconstituted to provide for full resumption of parenting. Friends are recognized and acknowledged in more profound ways. The legal mandates for sharing time with the children take on new meaning and pose still additional challenges.

Resolution also addresses the issue of the changing relationship with the extended family of the former spouse. This is also a period to reflect on personal roots, inherited values, and traditional beliefs.

As movement is made toward ultimate recovery, new risks are taken toward self-actualization. Dating begins. Personal interests are allowed some priority. The atmosphere is, on the whole, quite stimulating.

Suggestions for working through the stage of resolution:

1. Make time to pursue personal interests. "Me-Time" is essential for the personal growth necessary to function as an independent and successful adult.
2. Attend groups such as Parents Without Partners, church or synagogue singles groups, etc. These provide opportunities to discuss relevant issues and to meet potential new friends and dates.
3. Continue to write in your journal. Nothing is as reassuring as noting the continual progress in the journey through divorce.
4. Get enough rest, especially as activities expand. Often the frenzy of work and play leave too little time to recharge the physical stamina needed for the resolution stage.
5. Let friends know that you are ready to "meet someone". Be receptive to blind dates arranged by trusted friends. Even if you feel insecure and shy at first, make every effort to resume a social life. Each new excursion will provide an expanding repository of experience from which to draw in establishing a viable single life-style.
6. Budget monies for entertainment. Investment in the self is in order and will benefit the entire family.
7. Begin entertaining in your home. You feel self-conscious at first but this is a critical reentry requisite for taking charge of your life.
8. Create new traditions and new memories for yourself and your family. Celebrating holidays and birthdays will call for innovation. Think of special ways to brighten lonely times.
9. If you find yourself still unable to acknowledge friendships, to be a friend, or if you are still unable to socialize despite the encouragement of trusted confidants, consider seeking therapy for an interim period. Individual

and group therapy can facilitate movement toward full recovery. (See Case History IV.)

Suggestions for friends and relatives:

1. This is a period of letting go. The dependency needs will lessen, and your friend will require more freedom to explore single life. Recognize that this will be a loss for you—albeit in a good cause.
2. Be certain holidays and birthdays and anniversaries are not spent alone.
3. Encourage your friend to join new social groups.
4. Be supportive when she goes on her first date. This is an extremely important step forward into the social world.
5. Invite your friend out to share in shopping, dinner, and entertainment.
6. Intervene when you observe that your friend is over-extending herself.
7. Express admiration for courageous efforts, for example, going to a singles party for the first time, avoiding any "Poor you" tinge; compliment her social skills—grace, tact, wit—as if she is *enviable*.

5

STAGE FIVE

Recovery

EMERGING INDEPENDENCE

My life will be full again,
    even without your presence
I will laugh at jokes,
    cry for joy, hear music
    once more
Even though you are no longer here.

My body will awaken to
    the delights of sensation
I will revel in the
    tenderness of another's touch
Knowing that you kept me
    from enjoying so much.

Thank you for my freedom
I didn't want it then
I only wanted you—
But now I can clearly see that

my future happiness can
only be secure without
you.

Emerging Independence

At last the joys of life are opening up again and filling the conscious desires. Psychodynamically, in depression and withdrawal, it is impossible to take pleasure in what ordinarily generates happiness. Jokes are not as funny; music makes one cry. Smiles are forced; there is a constant veil of sadness and fear that screens out the joy.

Once the recovery stage is reached, smiles come more easily and laughs more spontaneously. Tears can still be shed, but this time for joy as well as grief. Time and life are preparing the script in which another person enters your world and responds to you.

The former spouse is being purged from the daily life with a calmness that indicates the release is indeed real. No longer does happiness depend on that person's participation in the marriage bed. He has been excluded, and the circle of new friends and relationships begins to open and widen as dignity and self-confidence reemerge.

A Triumph

The days seem filled
The nights not so long
The weekends not so desolate
The divorce no longer all wrong.

My life is getting back on track
My directions tho uncharted
    no longer as frightening
I'm growing content within
    myself
My senses ever heightening.

The world looks hopeful
It's good to survive
My destiny is *mine*
        to create and direct
Thank God I'm alive.

A TRIUMPH

The stage of recovery carries the work of resolution through to triumph. This poem describes that triumph in terms of ultimate peace in an uncoupled life. There is a spirit of the true joy of living.

Importantly, there is no longer the frenzy to catch up or indiscriminately fill time with activities to avoid being alone. Private moments are now cherished as opportunities for reflection and self-discovery.

A Triumph presents a person in full control of senses and faculties, equipped and ready to meet any challenge: "My destiny is mine." Survival is no longer an issue. The divorce is no longer the vector of absolute adversity.

Victory is at hand in positive attitude, expectation of oneself, and regard for the outside world. Indeed, the world that once cast an opaque cloud now welcomes you with unclouded horizons. Repatriation in the human race is now complete.

The stage of recovery is further defined by the ability to make those good memories on which to build an even more positive attitude for the future. *Triumph,* therefore, proclaims both an inner achievement in self-image and an external accomplishment in presupposing a productive liaison with the outside world.

THANK YOU

I needed to meet you
        needed to know you were there
I was afraid no one would
        like the unmarried me

I was afraid there was no one
  I would like
I wanted less than a torchy
  romance
I wanted more than a casual
  friend
You helped me feel secure
  that I am OK
You helped me on my road
  to becoming me
Thank you.

THANK YOU

Thank You introduces the new relationship that affirms you as an individual important to other adults. This is neither a rebound relationship nor a romantic interlude. This is a friendship with a member of the opposite sex affirms trust and openness to risk taking. Advice is mutually sought. Dreams and even nightmares are shared for exploration and interpretation.

Going out with a special friend continues throughout the stage of recovery. Self-affirmation demands positive experience over a sustained period of time. Several good dating friendships will contribute measurably to one's self-esteem and self-confidence.

Control is a key issue in a new relationship. One needs to know that one is in control emotionally, intellectually, and sexually. The poem implies that there is still apprehensiveness of getting involved in a situation from which you will not be able to extricate yourself. Yet there is the driving need to forge new connections.

How fortunate it is, then, to find at least one safe dating friendship. This is a prototype and model of future, mutually important relationships.

The expression of appreciation for what this relationship provides may be shared with your special friend, though it need not be. The most important consideration is that you are truly aware of what the relationship counts for in the measure of personal growth.

LOOK OUT FOR REBOUNDS

Watch your step girl—
You can't always see the
    stones in your path
Be careful—
If you trip, pick yourself
    up
Brush yourself
    off
Check the wisdom of your direction
And get going!

LOOK OUT FOR REBOUNDS

Life is in tempo again. Each day seems to be more interesting and exciting than the one before. This is a release phenomenon. There appear to be more rewards for attempting new activities than sitting in the home which was the bastion of security in the days when you were so steeped in self-pity. This is a sign of more full-fledged reentry on to the often convoluted pathways of the world at large. The risks are not as threatening and frightening as before; in fact, they may at times not seem like risks at all.

The recovery process capitalizes on the awareness that living in the real world can be more rewarding than living in the safety of fantasies. This poem is an assertion of the confidence and capacity to meet any novel situation, examine alternate directions, and choose in one's own best interests.

The frenzy of activities coupled with the need to reaffirm one's sexual identity are hallmarks of this part of the journey. However, a clear note of caution is sounded here on the dangers of rebound relationships. These early commitments are especially luring because the vivid recall of the desolation of being alone combines with the reminiscent joys and security of being coupled, to make for an almost uncontrollable propelling force.

The certainty of weekend plans and no more awkward first dates often precipitate disastrous alliances which have no future. *Look Out for Rebounds* warns that haste and failure to look ahead will lead to blunders. It also counsels recognizing and acknowl-

edging a mistake, by which one then cannot come off the loser.
New loves should be forged from personal strengths, not weaknesses.

Is a New Relationship Worth It?

The fear of abandonment
        surges through me
Tremors of hurt and pain
        rock my once stilled soul
Insecurity engulfs me

Pain is not a stranger to me
        loneliness is now an unknown
Yet I fear the known—
        fear some future hurt

I have to tremble
        You have hurt me so
I cannot suppress the
        agonizing fear of being
left
alone
again

I must face the inevitable—
        my future

Not precipitate it
Simply live today and then
        tomorrow will come
        and I will be there
        no matter
        what.

Is a New Relationship Worth It?

Recovery may be the final station in the journey through
divorce, but there are miles of track ahead. Challenges that must

be met and decisions that must be made by all mature adults continue to face you. If you are newly single, you will be confronted with deciding "Is a new relationship worth it?"

Universally, the risks of living and loving are constantly being evaluated. Problems in new relationships are frightening for all, especially if there is a history of loss. New relationships can stir the ashes of the dead relationship, and the hot coals of fear, distrust, and insecurity are all too easily rekindled to flare up and consume a fragile new friendship. This is the precarious time of rebirth as a loving human being.

Those who study human behavior unanimously agree that man is gregarious instinct, quality of life and longevity itself are correlated positively with man living in relationship to another human being. Unequivocally, a relationship with another—well chosen—has sustaining value and is worth the risks.

Autonomy and independence are personal assets, but need to be tempered with trust and acceptance of others. Having experienced loss and chaos and then a hard-won inner peace, one is understandably wary of new intimacies which may disturb the balance.

"Freedom" and "space" became words invoked to maintain safe distancing from those who offer the possibility of sharing love and life. For certain stages early in the journey through divorce those terms served a protective function, allowing wounds time to heal. Now such guardedness may cut one off from new fulfillment.

Is a New Relationship Worth It? asks the question and owns the fear of another rejection, but presses on with a strong "I will be there/no matter what"—the attitude achieved in the stage of recovery.

PENDULUM—WHO'S IN CHARGE?

I feel better tonight
The feelings in me
    are calmer
The ability to cope
    reemerging
My balance reestablishing
    itself.

Although he moves me to anger
Although he moves me to tears
Although he moves me to lose my temper

He does not move me.

PENDULUM—WHO'S IN CHARGE?

It is unreasonable to expect that there will never be painful reminders of what once was or what might have been. However, these emotional fluctuations through recall of the past and questions about uncertain future indicate increased *self-awareness*—a newfound resiliency. Growth proceeds when there is acceptance of these moodswings and the realization that they are part of the divorce process.

"Although he moves me to anger . . . to tears . . . to lose my temper . . ." is a direct admission that there are vulnerable points in the personality structure where a touch can trigger highly charged responses. Because of the intimacies that were shared for so many years, the ex-spouse "knows how to get to you." But while aware that one is open to attack, one has reached the point of being able to say, "He does not move me." At long last, control is no longer all in the hands of the former spouse. He still has the power to hurt, but not to demolish.

In this early phase of recovery, the mechanism is still sensitive and the pendulum may swing erratically. As time goes on, while its rhythm will occasionally be irregular, the trend is toward dependable equilibrium.

STRANGERS

You are a stranger to me now
I notice your shortcomings
        and wonder if I'd seen them
        before
I am amused at your awkwardness
        in talking to me
I am a stranger to you now.

Once we moved in rhythm
    listening to the blended
    beating of our hearts
Knowing that the rhythm
    could never be interrupted.
Yet today, because of man's
    capricious whims
    we are in discord.

We are strangers now.

STRANGERS

In every marriage, to some degree, there is a fantasy of the idealization of the spouse. The partner is deified and put on a pedestal to be adored and revered. To end the marital relationship and sever the bonds the spouse must be deidealized. The time has come to realize that the god has feet of clay.

The separateness that now prevails has provided a release from the other person. His shortcomings are very noticeable. Frailties and weaknesses that were once overlooked are now easily recognized. The spouse has become an ordinary man, with all of his mundane faults.

While all of the ramifications of becoming two separate people, no longer linked to each other are not yet clear, the dyad is broken. The intimacies and feelings once shared are being replaced by the distancing civilities and strained conventionalities unique to the divorce process. Neither casual strangers nor affectionate friends, the former spouses encounter the awkward, often poignant, dynamics of this changed relationship. This is indeed a sober statement of a human reality.

SURVIVAL

I am a survivor
I know that now—
I survived the emotional traumas
    and verbal assaults

I survived for three reasons
  my son
  my daughter and
  Me.

SURVIVAL

Not only is this poem a victory declaration of the ability to survive, but it is also an abbreviated chronicle of the journey through the divorce process. At first the need to keep the marriage vows intact was the compelling force. Dignity and self-respect were shed in a desperate attempt to save the fragile relationship. The vulnerabilities so exposed by the intimate knowledge of each other were explosives used to keep a dialogue going, regardless of the pain. Survival was an imponderable, and there seemed to be no reason to attempt to survive on one's own.

The ever-increasing inner *resolve* to survive, discovery of personal strengths, and the determination to parent effectively have led to the ultimate disengagement from the former spouse. "The verbal assaults and emotional traumas" have lost their impact. Survival is no longer a question; it has become fact.

WHEN?

My eyes are burning still from
    the tears
I can't still the anguish that
    swept over me
Your extravagances at my
    expense pain me
Yet I know I *will* be OK.

Perhaps someday the anger
    will abate
Perhaps someday the hurt
    will cease

Perhaps someday the pain
will be numb
But till then I still know
I'll be OK.

WHEN?

Unlike loss from the death of a loved one, loss as a result of divorce provides unlimited opportunities to come face to face with the object of grief. The mourning process is repeatedly interrupted, not by cherished memories, but by painful reminders of a presence no longer desired or wanted. These interruptions can still hurt, but they no longer have the power to devastate.

Monetary issues also have to be reconciled during the entire journey through divorce, but especially during the stage of recovery when you are settling into relatively permanent patterns of living. More than half of all divorced fathers fail to provide adequately for their children financially; nearly the same number fail to adequately provide for their children emotionally, with diminishing contact and interest.

When? alludes to the differential in earning power between divorced men and women. "Your extravagances at my expense pain me" is a biting observation which reminds us that the standard of living for the ex-wife generally falls substantially while that for the ex-husband generally rises significantly.

Pragmatically, two separately cannot live as well as two individually. Resources present and future will likely never follow parallel courses. Recovery implies you are prepared to face the discrepancies in earning power and resources. His extravagant gifts to the children can be manipulative to assuage guilt. His flaunting a financially liberated life-style—at her expense—may well incite jealousy, envy, and cynicism.

You are well advised to live within your means, and not to attempt to compete materially. There are more important dimensions to the quality of life where sincerity, loving devotion, and integrity of purpose will more than rise to the practical occasion. Furthermore, you can be assured that children can always distinguish the genuine from the gesture.

THE EMBER

The fire is flickering now
    the last flame struggling to continue
    disappearing from view and
    reemerging briefly

My strength is like the last
    flames of the evening fire
Struggling, smoldering, and
    silent
No longer strong, solid,
    and straight

But unlike the fire I will
    not become an ember
I will survive, stronger than before

Aware of my own resources
Never to be smothered.

THE EMBER

Recovery not only signifies an enduring survival, but it also heralds the ability to assess inner strengths and weaknesses. No longer a victim, it is now possible to continually evaluate and redefine the direction life is taking. Internal resolve has become your permanent partner on life's journey.

Another important aspect of this poem is the felt sense of self-accomplishment. Not only will life go on without the former partner, but the once despairing and immobilized woman will go forward "stronger than before."

The Ember emphatically states that there is no lingering doubt that existence without the mate is possible. Here survival is defined in terms of potency and replenishment rather than of meagerness. The thrust of this poem is that no man can smother a flame that refuses to be extinguished. Recovery is not to be trodden down. The stage of recovery is rather one of readiness to meet any challenge, unhampered by the old shackles, and fortified by personal attributes and skills.

IN THE SHADOWS

The despair flows through me
My body rocks with the
　　　　anguish
My soul is tortured with the
　　　　pain
My heart is torn with the
　　　　loss.

Where is the sunshine
Where are the flowers
Where is the quietly flowing brook
When will I find them again?

My life remains riveted
　　　　to the past tonight
Hoping for the return of those
　　　　gifts I cherish
　　　　peace
　　　　calm
　　　　tranquility and
　　　　love.

IN THE SHADOWS

The psyche does not heal according to strict theoretical guidelines but rather at an undulating pace over time. Stranded in the desert of despair, the spirit finds little purpose or meaning to counter to the sense of futility. The loss of the mate is a global one: it changes everything.

In every depression there is loss. During the journey through divorce, the identification of that loss proceeds as a matter of natural progression with an eye toward effectively compensating each deficit. To feel robbed of peace, serenity, and love is un-expectable. These reflections will continue throughout this stage of recovery as well.

Other losses may have the same paralyzing effect as the loss of the spouse. The loss of a newly formed relationship may shatter hopes and dreams for a new, coupled future. Unfortunately, it is not unusual to group similar losses together—only to compound the pain. Psychiatrically, this is a negative anamnestic response. It is much like the body's immunologically protective response to a booster injection.

Another cause of recrudescence of former feelings may be a personal tragedy such as the death of a beloved member of the former family. Celebrations that exclude you because you are no longer a member of that family likewise can stir painful feelings which reflect the felt loss. The former spouse may get sick, and now there is truly nothing you can do.

In the Shadows illustrates how in the midst of recovery there can be time-limited flashbacks. These do not thwart the forward thrust of this stage. It is therapeutic to identify these feelings as transient. "My life remains riveted to the past tonight"; but this feeling will not last. Things will look different in the morning.

JOGGING

I watch the joggers through my window
Wondering if they know where they are going
    as they pound the pavement
    puff and pant
    swelter and sweat
I wonder if feeling healthy and
    keeping in shape
Involves an element of suffering
    a modicum of pain
    a desire to persevere
    a personal triumph
Perhaps jogging and surviving divorce
    are really the same
It's the daily outings that
    finally create the fitness.

JOGGING

Recovery demands self-discipline much like that of an athlete's. The "high" that runners experience is not unlike the exhilaration that one feels in recovering from divorce. Each requires personal goal-setting, dedication, constant evaluation of progress, and perseverence, as well as life-style accommodation.

Psychiatrically, self-discipline characteristically involves increased capacity to delay gratification in exchange for attainment of more substantive objectives. Likewise, rational thinking takes precedence over primarily pleasure-oriented activities. This is frequently the litmus test for maturity.

By the time one has moved through the stage of recovery, there are already in place such skills as the ability to analyze minutely, compare multiple solutions, and set short-term as well as long-term goals. Decision making is predicated on a logic that is no longer prejudiced by emotions. Still there is plenty of scope for spontaneity and adventure.

Jogging articulates this commitment to win through self-discipline and perseverence—critical factors for survival. The strength builds from the cumulative impact of daily engagement. The happiness comes from the triumphs over these engagements.

THE NIGHT IS NO LONGER MY ENEMY

The night closes in around me
    blanketing the windows with darkness
The moon and stars pierce the blackness
    and illuminate the earth
Permitting celestial beams to
    brighten the dark.

Even enveloped in the evening
I am content within myself
I am a whole person now,
Complete within myself
Continuing to grow

>   to discover the joys of life
>   too easily taken for granted
>   to unfold my layers and
>   redefine my desires
>
>   The night is no longer my enemy
>   It offers me peace, tranquility, and hope.

THE NIGHT IS NO LONGER MY ENEMY

Another signpost of the stage of recovery is the recognition of felt security at those times and under conditions previously associated with tormenting thought, despair, and haunting loneliness. To be content within the self when evening comes is in sharp contrast to the earliest days of the journey when night and death were not so dissimilar.

The Night Is No Longer My Enemy signifies a renewal of the ability to profit consciously from emotional release: The quiet pleasure of solitude is heightened by an awareness of the associated personal growth. The healing process, curiously enough, becomes increasingly obvious.

As you begin to take more control of your life and destiny, you become more interested in process. Rightfully, you find pleasure in identifying the obstacles as they crumble. Simultaneously, you are appreciatively aware of the more routine joys of life that had been taken for granted. Hopes are solidly grounded in preparation, primed for opportunity. The differentiated sense of self inspires qualities of leadership. Finally, the healthy ego takes pleasure in natural beauty, especially when the natural beauty is from within.

GREAT EXPECTATIONS—SMALL DISAPPOINTMENTS

>   I expect too much
>   I expected not to miss the kids
>   I expected to be with him more
>   I expected to be continuously happy
>   I expected sunshiny days

I found that I miss the kids
I found that I was with him less
I found that I am sometimes very sad
I found that there are clouds in my days

But
I expect I will learn to deal with the
kids' absence
I expect I will learn I can't depend
on him to fill up my time and space
I expect I will learn that happiness
needs to be balanced with reality
I expect I will learn that clouds
can provide shade on sunshiny days

I expect I will be just fine.

GREAT EXPECTATIONS—SMALL DISAPPOINTMENTS

The stage of recovery may include moments of panic as new
life experiences present themselves. Finding someone new is unfortunately often seen as the panacea for divorce. That new relationship becomes the escape hatch from the daily trials of living
alone or as a single parent. Insight is necessary to realize that
another love per se will not solve problems; however, and more
promisingly, another love can add a dimension to a life that is
already in control.

There is also the continual process of adapting to less parenting time than the life cycle clock was supposed to allocate.
Weekends without the children may seem unnatural and leave
you with a lost feeling. This adjustment is difficult to make. Often
the lonely hours without the children are crammed with activity
to fill the sudden long gaps of free time. Well-meaning friends
will remark how lucky to be free of responsibility—but these
words fall mockingly on the haunting quiet of the house.

Ultimately, there is the real knowledge that no perfect solutions to life's problems exist. There is only the realization that
each day must be lived to its fullest, savoring the sweet and swal-

lowing the bitter. Because no life is in total harmony, it follows that divorce should not be made the scapegoat.

This poem is primarily a declaration of self-sufficiency. Ego functioning is in an expanding state. Despite the risks and the natural tendency to respond to new people in an overly determined manner, the conclusion is optimistic: Disappointments are inevitable, but the great expectations are of *oneself,* and are therefore in good hands. "I expect I will be just fine."

It Still Hurts

> Over a year
>> and where am I?
>>> still hurting
>>> still afraid
>>> still alone
>
> I can't run away from our past
>> our children prevent it
>> so I
>>> still see you
>>> still see your family
>>> still see the anger
>
> I can't look into my future
>> so I find I am
>>> still frightened
>>> still anguished
>>> still confused
>
> Over a year—
>> and damn it
> Where am I?

It Still Hurts

Anniversary recall of traumatic events is an ancient tradition, dating back to biblical days. Therapists refer to anniversary reactions in describing the eruption of turbulent feelings of pain, anguish, and confusion—seemingly long laid to rest—on the calendaric date of a significant loss.

The time line is not the same for all people. The anniversary of divorce can fall at any stage of the journey. Whether one is still in the stage of depression, anger, resolution, or recovery will make a strong difference.

In the stage of recovery, the anniversary reaction needs to be understood as a marker of the continuous passage of time. It denotes the increasing distance between yesterday's catastrophic experience and today's independent living.

In the midst of a long personal success record, an anniversary reaction still can strike and can last for moments or sometimes for days. This is not an indicator of relapse. It is no cause for a sense of defeat. It only points up that time does *not* heal all wounds. The journey through divorce is a long and arduous process initially begun as a survival course and ultimately continued as a mode of celebrating life.

It Still Hurts reminds one that the what-ifs and the if-onlys will naturally come to mind on anniversary dates. Remember too that for the anniversary of the death of a marriage there is no official verdict, no eulogy, no epitaph. This is one more day just like any other, a link in an ongoing progression, not to be sacrificed on the altar of the past.

THE CAROUSEL

I'm reaching out again
    my arms are stretching
    my fingers extended
Grasping to touch
    happiness
Trying to catch
    the world
    the people
    the good times
    the fun

Afraid my reach might
　　not be quite long
　　enough
　　or strong enough

But I am reaching out again
I will try.

THE CAROUSEL

No longer intimidated by the fear of venturing out, life becomes an intoxicating adventure. The decision has been made to reach out and embrace all that life can offer. "I am reaching out again, I will try" announces the rejoining of the forces of the world.

Psychiatrically, one recovers by moving through stages of progressive challenge and risk-taking, building on newly developed strengths. To lament weaknesses is to remain immobilized. With mushrooming successes courage is gained to cut new paths. Each conquest of new ground enlarges the repertoire of successful coping techniques that serve to make the journey a little smoother.

The race for the merry-go-round, suggesting the vitality and eagerness of childhood, when one couldn't bear to get left behind, is the symbol of the energy of the recovered adult, now primed to jump aboard and grab for the brass ring, win or miss.

AM I THAT WOMAN WHO WAS TREMBLING WITH FEAR?

Am I that woman who was trembling with fear
　　Afraid to face the day
　　Terrified of the long nights
　　Frightened to be alone?

Today I am a woman trembling with happiness
　　Enjoying each day
　　living each night, often finding them too short

conquering the fear of being alone
Proud to be me
Alive, well and free.

I am certain that I can meet my future
    greet it with confidence
    face the unknowns and master them
    reach out across any despair
    and survive.

Am I that woman who was trembling with fear?

Am I That Woman Who Was Trembling with Fear?

Pride surges through this poem. Beyond survival, the image in the mirror shows a rediscovered ability to enjoy pleasure. Nothing is guaranteed, but there is confidence that the unknowns can be mastered and the ghosts of the past laid to rest.

The journey through divorce has been laborious. There were no shortcuts, few trade-offs, and no anesthetic for the pain. The metamorphosis is now complete from being one half of a dyadic relationship, in which survival meant being inextricably bound, to a new autonomous being who stands on her own. The ending is one of ongoing achievement, hope, joy, and expectation of still brighter days and more deeply peaceful nights. Divorce was the challenge. Renewed life is the victory.

The journey through divorce has ended. The competent, hopeful, independent, single individual is now on course in the mainstream of life.

Case History V

Nancy and Richard, both in their early thirties, were married for 10 years and had two children when Richard abruptly terminated the marriage. Nancy found herself unexpectedly having to raise an infant and a three-year-old, work full time, and journey through divorce. At the time of her divorce Nancy was living in a city where her only family were her in-laws. It soon became apparent that at traditional family gatherings Nancy was now awkwardly excluded. Holidays were lonely and painful.

Nancy worked through the stages of denial, depression, and anger fairly completely before she reached a monumental decision; namely, to move 2,000 miles to where she had supportive family members. Nancy established for herself and her children a new home built on the hopes and visions of a brighter future. She ultimately found satisfactory employment, began to develop rewarding friendships and discovered for the first time since the divorce a contentment within herself.

Friends, old and new, and members of her immediate family lent sustaining emotional support over the ensuing months. This allowed Nancy to effectively confront the long agenda of residual problems.

As would be expected, short-lived regressive episodes arose, with temptations of reconciliation, moving back, and rebound relations. As Nancy progressed through the stage of recovery she was able to select men who were more compatible with her ideals and long-term goals.

Commentary:

The regaining of balance and the ability to interact and enjoy relationships that are of value and growth-inducing are the signposts of the stage of recovery. Regaining health does not necessarily imply remarriage, although this frequently occurs. Recovery does, however, imply that one is happy with one's lot and that one feels a certain control over the direction that life is taking, much to the satisfaction of that individual. This is the essence of that inner peace with which one crosses the wire at the end of the pilgrimage through divorce and takes up the common human journey.

SUMMARY AND SUGGESTIONS

Recovery is a triumph for life: The major issues of the stage of resolution have been won. One is at peace with oneself and knows what one is able to bear and to do. The external world is no longer hedged with shadowy perils poised to spring on you at every turn. Instead, the world beams on the hopeful with opportunities for new learning, new roles, possibilities undreamed of earlier.

New relationships not only shed new light on self-scrutiny but fit into an overall purpose. There is satisfaction in being uncoupled as well as in being involved with important others. Nights are no longer threatening; solitude is a welcomed chance for reflection and fueling.

The renascence of the self in the stage of recovery includes self-affirmation as a social and sexual being. Authentic power is realized in the reaching out to engage on many levels, including social activities, work and avocational interests, and cultural pursuits.

Finances are encompassed within the uncompetitive reality of your settled circumstances. Steady self-discipline and patience continue to pay off.

The emergent and secure self finds renewed ability to take pleasure in the simple joys of life. Horizons are expanding, stimulating new ideas and interests.

Reality is clearly focused in the stage of recovery. The realization that there are no perfect solutions nor absolutely fair compromises accepts the momentary reflections on past loss even in the course of years that have been crowned with success. Anniversary reactions are recognized as normal and are kept in perspective.

Finally, you are a complete and competent person with an abiding faith in yourself and your future. The journey through divorce has not proved a deadend or a detour as you come out on the main lane.

Suggestions for the Recovery Stage of Divorce:

1. Although you may have finished this book before completing your personal journey, it will be helpful to review *Journey through Divorce* and note those poems and narratives that especially speak to you. As you meet with obstacles that seem to impede your progress, go back and reread those marked passages. This may help you formulate new strategies.

2. Record in your journal moments of happiness and pleasure that replenish your memory bank.
3. Now that things are going so much better, avoid sabotaging your gains. Catch yourself up when leery of good times with such comments as "This can't be real . . . This can't last . . ." Visualize yourself writing these words on a piece of paper and then throwing them in the trash where they belong.
4. There will still be times when you will experience sadness because of your loss. These occasions mean you are a feeling, live person. Your past meant something, which is why your future does.
5. Continue to build a support system of friends. Don't sacrifice these ties to a new dating relationship that may or may not endure.
6. Be cautious about remarrying. Rebound relationships are most frequent when the desire to remarry is stronger than the desire to "make it on your own."
7. Accept compliments graciously. That way you'll get more. Take it one step further: Compliment yourself.
8. Be proud of yourself!

Suggestions for friends and family:

1. Continue to be a sounding board for your friend. Listening in a supportive and nonjudgmental manner is a powerful intervention in its own right.
2. Be patient if it seems like the stage of recovery is taking too long. Remember that each person has her own timeline. You can't hurry it up.
3. Try not to introduce the topic of the ex-spouse and the attendant losses when no predicate has been laid for this.
4. Continue to include your friend in the usual family and social activities. Remind your friend also to include you on her festive occasions.
5. Feel free to exchange ideas and criticisms. Handling your friend with kid gloves would only serve to perpetuate the myth that she is weak and fragile. Recovery reflects parity.

EPILOGUE

SCRAPBOOK

Our life together
    seems like an old memory
A scrapbook in the
    pages of time
Where we began as children
    and grew into adults.

But when I turn the pages
    in my mind
I hardly recognize the
    woman
    who stares up at me
She has changed so much
    in so little time

Oh—I remember
    I really do—
    but the time
        has let you go
        and let me go

And I am ready to
    fill the next book.

BIBLIOGRAPHY

ADULT

Andrew, J. *Divorce and the American family.* New York: Franklin Watts, 1978.

Atkin, E., & Rubin, E. *Part-time father.* New York: Vanguard Press, 1976.

Cook, A., & McBride, J. Divorce: Helping children cope. *School Counselor,* 1982, *30*(2), 88–94.

Epstein, J. *Divorced in America.* New York: Dutton, 1974.

Fisher, B. *Rebuilding when your relationship ends.* San Luis Obispo, Calif: Impact, 1986.

Gardner, R. *The parents' book about divorce.* New York: Doubleday, 1977.

Goldstein, E. *Ego psychology and social work practice.* New York: Free Press, 1984.

Jacobson, E. *The self and the object world.* New York: International Universities Press, 1964.

Jewett, C. *Helping children cope with separation and loss.* Boston: Harvard Common Press, 1982.

Krantzler, M. *Creative divorce.* New York: Signet, 1974.

Krantzler, M. *Learning to love again.* New York: Bantam, 1979.

Kushner, H. *When bad things happen to good people.* New York: Schocken, 1981.

Lederer, W., & Jackson, D. *The mirages of marriage.* New York: W. W. Norton, 1968.

Madow, L. *Anger: How to recognize and cope with it.* New York: Scribner's, 1972.

Masterson, L. *The real self: A developmental self and object relations approach.* New York: Brunner/Mazel, 1986.

Napolitane, C., & Pellegrino, V. *Living and loving after divorce.* New York: Signet, 1977.

Sager, C. *Marriage contracts and couple therapy.* New York: Brunner/Mazel, 1976.

Shapiro, J., & Caplan, M. *Parting sense: A complete guide to divorce Mediation.* Maryland: Greenspring, 1986.

Tafford, A. *Crazy time: Surviving divorce.* New York: Bantam, 1984.

Wallerstein, J., & Kelly, J. *Surviving the breakup: How children and parents cope with divorce.* New York: Basic Books, 1980.

Watzlawick, P., Weakland, J., & Fisch, R. *Change: Principles of problem formation and problem resolution.* New York: W. W. Norton, 1974.

Weiss, R. *Marital separation.* New York: Basic Books, 1975.

Yalom, I. *The theory and practice of group psychotherapy.* New York: Basic Books, 1985.

Yardley, K., & Honess, T. *Self and identity psychosocial perspectives.* New York: John Wiley & Sons, 1987.

CHILDREN

Berger, T. *How does it feel when your parents get divorced?* New York: J. Messner, 1977.

Boeckman, C. *Surviving your parents' divorce.* New York: F. Watts, 1980.

Gardner, R. *The boys and girls book about divorce.* New York: Bantam, 1970.

Gardner, R. *The boys and girls book about one parent families.* New York: Bantam, 1978.

Gilbert, S. *How to live with a single parent.* New York: Lothrop, Lee & Shephard, 1982.

Hazen, B. *Two homes to live in: A child's-eye view of divorce.* New York: Human Science Press, 1978.

Klein, N. *Taking sides.* New York: Avon, 1974.

Le Shan, E. *What's going to happen to me? When parents separate or divorce.*
New York: Four Winds Press, 1978.

Sinberg, J. *Divorce is a grown-up problem.* New York: Avon, 1978.

Stein, S. *On divorce: An open family book for parents and kids together.* New
York: Walker, 1979.

White, A. *Divorce.* New York: F. Watts, 1979.

COMMUNITY RESOURCES

Professional

American Psychiatric Association
1400 K Street, N.W.
Washington, D.C. 20005

American Psychological Association
1200 17 Street, N.W.
Washington, D.C. 20036

American Group Psychotherapy Association
25 East 21 Street, 6th Floor
New York, N. Y. 10010

American Orthopsychiatric Association Inc.
19 West 44 Street, Suite 1616
New York, New York

Counselors

American Association for Counseling and Development
5999 Stevenson Avenue
Alexandria, Virginia 22304

American Association of Sex Educators, Counselors and
Therapists
Eleven Dupont Circle, N. W.
Suite 220
Washington, D.C. 20036

American Association of Marriage and Family Therapists
1717 K Street, N. W.
Washington, D.C. 20006

National Association of Social Workers
1425 H Street, N.W.
Washington, D.C. 20005

Clergy and Religious Agencies

Catholic:

National Conference of Catholic Charities
Call local parish

Protestant:

Joint Department of Family Life
National Council of the Churches of Christ
475 Riverside Drive
New York, N.Y. 10010

Jewish:

Association of Jewish Family & Children's Agencies
P. O. Box 248
Kendall Park, New Jersey 08824

Agencies

Family Service Agency
254 W. 31 Street
New York, N. Y. 10001

Organizations

Parents Without Partners, Inc.
7910 Woodmont Avenue
Washington, D.C. 20014
NOW
1957 East 73 Street
Chicago, Illinois 60649
Recovery, Inc.
Call Local Branch

Legal

The American Bar Association
750 North Lakeshore Drive
Chicago, Illinois 60611

The American Trial Lawyers Association
10535 31 Street N.W.
Washington, D.C. 20007

INDEX